# ETERNAL *by* CHOICE

## Only Those Who Believe in Christ Live Forever

ROBERT TAYLOR

Unless otherwise noted, Scripture taken from the New King James Version®. Copyright © 1982 by Thomas Nelson. Used by permission. All rights reserved.

Scripture quotations marked (ESV) are from The ESV® Bible (The Holy Bible, English Standard Version®), copyright © 2001 by Crossway, a publishing ministry of Good News Publishers. Used by permission. All rights reserved.

Scripture quotations marked (NASB®) are from the New American Standard Bible®, Copyright © 1960, 1971, 1977, 1995, 2020 by The Lockman Foundation. Used by permission. All rights reserved. www.lockman.org

Scripture quotations designated (NET) are from the NET Bible® copyright ©1996, 2019 by Biblical Studies Press, L.L.C. http://netbible.com All rights reserved. Scripture quoted by permission.

Scripture quotations marked (NIV) are from The Holy Bible, New International Version® NIV® Copyright © 1973 1978 1984 2011 by Biblica, Inc.™ Used by permission. All rights reserved worldwide.

Italics in scripture quotations have not been retained from the original. Italics are the author's own emphasis.

Unless otherwise noted, italics in quotations from reference works, commentaries, and other writers are from the original source cited.

Published by Sherwood Heritage Press
SherwoodHeritagePress@outlook.com

Hardback ISBN: 979-8-218-07992-5
Paperback ISBN: 979-8-218-07986-4
Ebook ISBN: 979-8-218-07987-1

Printed in the United States of America

*To my mom*

# CONTENTS

# PREFACE

*B*ack in 2001, a fresh look at what the Bible says about final judgment convinced me that perish, death, destruction, and burn up should be taken at face value. It wasn't until 2009, however, that I devoted myself to the biblical research I knew the evangelical world would want to see from anyone who advocated conditional immortality rather than the traditional view of hell. The result was *Rescue from Death* (Outskirts Press 2012). A couple of years later, I decided to do a more thorough edition of *Rescue from Death* (Dog Ear Publishing 2017), now *Rescue from Death: The Good News of John 3:16* (Sherwood Heritage Press 2021). I thought this would be the end of my book writing on conditionalism, and it well may have been if it wasn't for Doug Schaak.

I had sent three copies of the 2017 edition of *Rescue* to Multnomah University. One copy went to Doug Schaak as he was in charge of Multnomah's "Hot Topic" chapels. *Rescue from Death* was life-changing for Doug, bringing healing to his heart and his theology. With our busy schedules, it took a while for us to have much opportunity to talk, but that changed after Multnomah's school year ended in the spring of 2021. Our conversations included the benefits of a book that could reach a wider audience. I knew it would be great to have a more accessible presentation of conditional immortality because *Rescue from Death* ended up being so thorough that it was challenging to get through it, but with so much time already invested I had no plans to write another book. It took Doug's enthusiasm, encouragement, and unexpected offer to get me to writing again.

Doug has not only been part of Multnomah's faculty for a quarter-century, he is the director of the university's English Department. When he offered to be my editor, the opportunity was too good to turn down. It has been a great pleasure working with Doug and getting to know him. He's helped me become a better writer and *Eternal by Choice* a reality. This means so much to me because I believe *Eternal by Choice* is the book I was always meant to write.

Robert Taylor

## CHAPTER ONE

# THE CONFLICT WITHIN

*I*t's the fourth quarter. The score is tied. The noise in the stadium hits nearly 115 decibels as the quarterback drops back to pass. The receiver is just about to catch the football when a defender delivers a vicious hit, causing the receiver to fall to the turf where he lies motionless. Instantly, a hush comes over the stadium; grown men battling each other moments before drop to their knees in prayer; medics rush on to the playing-field, everyone watching for a sign of movement. No one wants this man to be paralyzed for life.

If an elderly person collapses in the church parking lot or someone breaks a leg or is hurt in an accident, the normal person rushes to help. We make sure the injured get the assistance they need because that's the way God made us. This is doubly true for Christians. In addition to being made in the image of God, believers are also born of God, and their "born-again DNA" includes meeting the needs of others. John writes,

> This is how we know what love is: Jesus Christ laid down his life for us. And we ought to lay down our lives for our brothers and sisters. If anyone has material possessions and sees a brother or sister in need but has no pity on them, how can the love of God be in that person? (1 Jn. 3:16–17, NIV)

Because believers instinctively desire to relieve distress, to contemplate the eternal suffering of fathers and mothers and sons and daughters creates an agonizing conflict. C. S. Lewis wrote that he detested hell "from the bottom of my heart."[1] Lewis refused to try to prove the doctrine tolerable, saying, "make no mistake; it is *not* tolerable."[2] J. I. Packer once asked, "Who can take pleasure in the thought of people being eternally lost?"[3] Packer went on to say that "If you want to see folks damned [forever in hell], there is something wrong with you."[4] In *Erasing Hell*, Francis Chan sides with the traditional, eternal conscious torment (ECT), view of hell, which prompts a confession by Chan that surely resonates with many:

> What causes my heart to ache right now as I'm writing this is that my life shows little evidence that I actually believe this [ECT]. Every time my thoughts wander to the future of unbelievers, I quickly brush them aside so they don't ruin my day.... We can talk about the fate of some hypothetical person, but as I look up and see their smiles, I have to ask myself if I really believe what I have written in this book.[5]

Think of someone you care about, and picture that person in agony; try to imagine that suffering going on forever without end. Your mind turns from the thought because it is contrary to the very core of your being. As John Stott famously said of ECT,

> Well, emotionally, I find the concept intolerable and do not understand how people can live with it without either cauterising their feelings or cracking under the strain.[6]

I'm convinced that this is the story of most Christians, whether they realize it or not. In order to maintain one's sanity and hold to the traditional doctrine of hell, Christians will adopt one coping mechanism or another. I know I can relate to Stott's words.

## MY OWN STORY

I grew up in a home where neither God nor religion was ever mentioned. Church was never discussed. Christmas was for presents. Easter was about chocolate bunnies and dyeing eggs to hide for my younger brothers. My only exposure to scripture came in the seventh grade when for a time I read some of the Psalms out of a pocket New Testament with Psalms and Proverbs given to me by the Gideons the previous year at my elementary school, a public school, believe it or not! It wouldn't be until after graduating from high school in 1969 that Christ would reach me.

A friend invited me to go on a youth retreat in the San Juan Islands of Washington State. Camping out on beautiful Orcas Island, I encountered a group of people who loved Jesus. The joyful spirit of these believers impressed me; they had a camaraderie that many of us who grew up in the Sixties longed to experience. By the end of the retreat, I wanted to know about Christ and sought out Richard, one of the leaders. As we waited for the ferry and rode it to the mainland, Richard shared from God's Word: "In the beginning was the Word, and the Word was with God, and the Word was God. And the Word became flesh and dwelt among us" (Jn. 1:1, 14). I listened intently to each verse, nodded, and wanted to hear more. "All have sinned and fall short of the glory of God" (Rom. 3:23); "Christ died for our sins according to the Scriptures, and that He was buried, and that He rose again the third day" (1 Cor. 15:3–4). No verse mentioned hell, and no trace of ECT was involved. The focus was on Jesus: who He was, what He had done for me, and that He wanted to come into my life.

In the ferry terminal on the mainland, I was still trying to take it all in as the time came for everyone to pile into cars for the trip home. Richard wanted to pray. It was the first time anyone had ever prayed for me in my presence. Waiting for the caravan to get on the road, I looked out over the water, the sun bright above the horizon, and the realization came over me that I was loved by God. I said to Him, "When I get home, I'm going to ask You into my life."

As a newborn believer with no background in Christianity, the first days and weeks were a bit up and down, but after about seven months I was all about Jesus, church, prayer, and the Bible. I had entered into a brand-new world and was eager to explore it. If the church doors were open, I was there. Our church had a strong evangelistic emphasis, and I repeatedly heard phrases such as "eternal separation from God" and "everyone must exist somewhere forever." These expressions eventually led me to see eternal conscious torment in the Bible.

Though I had blocked it out of my mind, looking back, I can remember when I first came to really understand the traditional view of hell. With the idea that everyone must live somewhere forever firmly planted in my mind, reading about the torment of the rich man in hell (Lk. 16:23, KJV), that hell is "fire that never shall be quenched" (Mk. 9:43, KJV), and of worms that don't die (Mk. 9:44), it looked like the Bible taught that the unsaved would suffer terribly forever. The thought was horrifying.

At that moment, the Bible seemed to paint a picture of Someone that I didn't recognize and couldn't imagine being close to. But having grown up in the world, I knew the world had no answers to life. I was somewhat familiar with Eastern religion and had found nothing there for me. As young as I was, I knew there was no alternative to the God who loved me so much that He sent His Son to die for my sins. With the pressure mounting, I considered further study of hell, but if other verses confirmed what I thought I was seeing, it would add to the stress that was already overwhelming me. It was an intense dilemma because God had done so much for me, and I wanted to follow Him.

A couple of months after accepting Christ, I was hit with doubts about God's reality; this was just before heading off to start college, where, unwisely, I briefly experimented with drugs. It was brief because my experience was a bad one. It felt like a series of explosions went off in my brain, and I was afraid that I had permanently damaged myself. Like the prodigal son, I came to my senses and knew that I needed God's help, but I still had doubts. Having moved back to my parents' home, I purposed to go to church each Sunday and spend five minutes a day reading the Bible. I figured this would give God a chance to work in my life. Not long afterwards, at the youth meeting that followed the Sunday evening service, the Lord worked through the message and renewed my faith. When I got home, everyone was in bed; I immediately dropped to my knees in the living room and started thanking God. I was telling Him all the things I now wanted to do when I felt something warm moving on the top front of my head and suddenly realized that I had been healed from the damage done by the drugs. It was completely unexpected, and I have no words for how blessed I felt. It was the pure grace of God, and it set me on fire for Him.

Growing up, as I mentioned, God was never discussed in our family. What I didn't know was that my father was an atheist and hostile toward Christianity. I must have had some sense of this, though, as I had hidden away the New Testament given to me by the Gideons without saying a word about it to anyone. When Dad realized that I had become a Christian, his anger was plain enough; even my returning from a mission trip with my long hair cut off didn't lessen his hostility. This helped make for an interesting summer of 1970.

Dad had recently become a contract trucker for Mayflower movers. Unhappy with the work and wages of the helpers he had to hire from city to city, he decided to take me with him on the road for a three-month trip. For me, to travel the country and work with Dad was a once-in-a-lifetime opportunity as a son and a new Christian, but it had its challenges. We worked seven days a week, taking only two weekends off while we were gone. In the evening and at night, Dad had the cab with a three-quarter bed. I slept in the trailer. Besides clothes, I had three things: a sleeping bag, a flashlight, and a Bible. Evening after evening for three months, it was me and the four walls of the trailer. I had never been so isolated, but I wasn't alone. Reading my Bible and singing hymns and praise songs, the presence of the Lord was with me.

I've told these stories because it's important to realize that we're dealing with so much more than a point of doctrine. We're talking about the Person we worship and have given our lives to, the One who is closer to us than a brother. To have my Savior associated with the endless suffering of fathers and mothers and sons and daughters was gut-wrenching. But I knew God to be good, and He had become everything to me, so I took the only option that seemed available: I compartmentalized ECT.

Imagine putting a family heirloom that you hated but couldn't part with in a spare room, locking the door, and throwing away the key. That's essentially what I did with ECT. If the Bible taught ECT, I couldn't disavow it, but I could, as much as possible, put it out of my mind. Thus began the emotional numbing of my heart.

This way of handling hell was easy to maintain in the evangelical community to which I belonged. In the fall of 1971, my hunger for the Word led me to the Multnomah School of the Bible, now Multnomah University.[7] During my three plus years there, we had open discussions on a variety of topics. Calvinism versus Arminianism was especially intense, but I don't recall a single discussion on hell. The same was true in seminary. I enrolled at Northwest Baptist Seminary toward the end of 1988, the year John Stott pleaded for "frank dialogue among Evangelicals" regarding hell, urging that "the ultimate annihilation of the wicked should at least be accepted as a legitimate, biblically founded alternative to their eternal conscious torment."[8] But I didn't hear about that in seminary; it wasn't mentioned in church, either. My wife and I moved quite a bit, and we fellowshipped with people from a variety of evangelical churches. Everywhere we went, ECT was in doctrinal statements; everyone knew it was the position of the church, but it wasn't a topic of conversation. I avoided the subject because I had compartmentalized hell, and the same was probably true for most Christians. When we did speak of the destiny of unbelievers, it was typically in terms of eternal separation from God and left at that. The longer this went on, the easier it got, and the more callous I became. After a while, I could talk about hell as if it were just another doctrine.

## Blind to the Conflict

Thirty years after accepting Christ, I had earned three degrees in biblical studies, including a doctorate, served as an adjunct faculty member of a Bible college, and led many church Bible study prayer groups, all in a theologically conservative context. I had also become closed-minded when it came to hell. In my experience, only atheists and theological liberals questioned ECT. In fact, during those thirty years I never heard a single Christian deviate from the traditional view of hell. When this finally happened, my reaction was quite revealing.

One day I overheard a good friend and Christian brother, George Brown, tell an unsaved colleague that the traditional view of hell wasn't true. And I thought to myself: *You can't take the easy way out. You have to take the difficult truths along with the great blessings of the Bible.* My knee-jerk reaction not only revealed that I had become closed-minded; the fact that I could so readily defend a doctrine that deep-down inside I hated shows how blind I had become to the conflict within me, now deeply suppressed. Then something unexpected happened that would change my life.

## A TURNING POINT

George and I were talking about Revelation 21:4, "And God will wipe away every tear from their eyes; there shall be no more death, nor sorrow, nor crying." George felt this indicated that in the new earth we won't remember loved ones who died without Christ. Then he commented, *God alone will bear that sorrow.* These words stopped me in my tracks.

In the evangelical circles in which I fellowshipped, the predominant understanding was that God's wrath toward unbelievers is eternal. Yet George spoke of God *mourning* the loss of those who had rejected Him. The contrast was so stark that it stunned me. The picture of the Father painted by George's words was consistent with the heart of God revealed in Jesus' lament over Jerusalem: "O Jerusalem, Jerusalem, the one who kills the prophets and stones those who are sent to her! How often I wanted to gather your children together, as a hen gathers her chicks under her wings, but you were not willing!" (Matt. 23:37). It was also consistent with Jesus' words at Calvary: "Father, forgive them, for they do not know what they do" (Lk. 23:34). Could it be that God didn't have eternal wrath for sinners? Could the traditional view of hell be wrong? At that moment, all I knew for sure was that I had been confronted with something that merited investigation. Like the Jews at Berea who responded to controversial teaching by diligently studying the scriptures (Acts 17:10–11), I determined to take a fresh, unbiased look at what God's Word had to say about the destiny of the unsaved. I would study the key biblical texts as if for the first time.

## WHAT I FOUND AMAZED ME

Beginning in Genesis, I reread the key verses related to hell; to my surprise, I discovered that they didn't actually say what I had been taught and what I had long assumed. Take the story of the rich man and Lazarus in Luke 16, for example.

My crisis with hell came when I was new to the faith, knew nothing about Greek or Hebrew, and before the NASB and most other modern versions of the Bible were available. So when my King James Bible said that the rich man was in torments in hell (Lk. 16:23), I took it at face value. But the setting of the story of the rich man and Lazarus isn't hell; it is Hades as the NKJV correctly states: "And being in torments in Hades, he lifted up his eyes and saw Abraham afar off, and Lazarus in his bosom."

## The Difference between Hades and hell

Hades and hell (*Gehenna*) are distinct words and represent distinct realities. Hell refers to the lake of fire. Hades is the New Testament equivalent of the Old Testament *Sheol*. Theologians refer to Hades/Sheol as the *intermediate state* because the unsaved reside there from biological death to the Day of Judgment (Rev. 20:11–13), which directly leads to the casting of the unsaved into the lake of fire (Rev. 20:15). Unfortunately, the KJV is not careful to distinguish between Hades/Sheol and hell. John Walvoord writes,

> In the Authorized Version, *Sheol* in the Old Testament and *Hades* in the New Testament are incorrectly translated by the English word *hell*. Both *Sheol* and *Hades* refer to the intermediate state or, as some believe, in certain instances to the grave. These terms *never* refer to the eternal state of punishment; therefore they should not have been translated in any instance by the word *hell*.[9]

Given the distinction between Hades and hell, it is disappointing that the KJV conflates these terms. This is not only a translation error but one that leads to a false understanding of final judgment. Perhaps there is anguish in Hades/Sheol for the unsaved prior to the judgment at the Great White Throne,[10] but if we want to know what ultimately happens to the unsaved in hell, we need to study passages that talk about hell. Luke 16:19–31 is not one of them. It has no bearing on the doctrine of final judgment one way or the other.

## NO WISHFUL THINKING HERE

Common sense and reason are essential to life and theology. God calls us to judge, discern, and test all things, but wishful thinking is a waste of time. Whatever the Bible teaches is the way things are going to be. Period. I'm interested in what the Bible actually says about hell, which convinced me that the traditional position was false. Not only do traditionalist proof texts fail to hold up under scrutiny, in the chapters ahead, we'll see that all of the explicit statements of scripture concerning the final destiny of unbelievers teach that the unsaved will ultimately be no more. Let's look at one example.

### The Testimony of John the Baptist

> His [Christ's] winnowing fan is in His hand, and
> He will thoroughly clean out His threshing floor, and
> gather His wheat into the barn; but He will burn up
> the chaff with unquenchable fire. (Matthew 3:12)

This key verse contains John the Baptist's warning of judgment to Pharisees and Sadducees whom John called, to their faces, a "brood of vipers" (Matt. 3:7). John's warning is built on the picture of a farming technique in which threshed wheat is tossed into the air with a shovel shaped like a fork. This is done so that the lighter chaff, the outer husk, might be blown away by the wind while the heavier edible wheat falls down to the threshing floor. John is saying, then, that Jesus will separate the wheat (the saved) from the chaff (the unsaved). The saved will be brought into Jesus' barn (kingdom), but the unsaved will be burned up.

Traditionalists readily recognize that the chaff is the unsaved and unquenchable fire the final judgment fire. Christopher Morgan states, "John the Baptist stresses the final separation of the righteous from the wicked, noting that the wicked will be thrown into hell and 'burned with unquenchable fire' (Matt. 3:1–12)."[11] Traditionalists typically emphasize banishment from the kingdom and say little about the chaff burning up in unquenchable fire. Students of the Word shouldn't dodge any text, but traditionalist avoidance in this case isn't hard to understand. The word for burn up (*katakaio*) in Matthew 3:12 has but one meaning, and it is devastating to the eternal suffering view.

Gingrich and Danker's *A Greek-English Lexicon of the New Testament*, W. E. Vine's *An Expository Dictionary of New Testament Words*, Alfred Marshall's *The Interlinear Greek-English New Testament*, Fritz Rienecker's *Linguistic Key to the Greek New Testament*, *The NET Bible*, *Strong's Exhaustive Concordance*, and *Thayer's Greek Lexicon* all define *katakaio* using terms such as burn up, burn utterly, consume, consume by fire, and completely burn up. Not only is there no other meaning for this word, there is no legitimate way to construe it to mean that the chaff eternally smolders.

Every time *katakaio* is used in the New Testament, something is burned to ashes, burned up, or utterly consumed (Matt. 13:30, 40; Acts 19:19; 1 Cor. 3:15; Heb. 13:11; 2 Pet. 3:10; Rev. 8:7, 17:16, 18:8). With only one meaning of the word and only one way the word is used in the New Testament, we have overwhelming certainty as to what will happen to the unsaved. Yet there is more confirmation: the chaff is consumed in *unquenchable* fire.

Starting and maintaining a fire can be a rigorous undertaking. Take something as burnable as an old dry log, lay it in a fireplace in a bed of newspaper, strike a match to it, and watch what happens: the flame sputters and dies out. It takes intense, sustained heat to kindle the log and start it burning, and it helps immensely if air is allowed to get underneath the log. Moreover, once the fire is going, it typically requires tending to keep it going. Why? Fire by nature is quenchable. Specific conditions are necessary to start and maintain a fire. The fire of Matthew 3:12, on the other hand, is "unquenchable fire," fire that is impervious to the obstacles to combustion.

John the Baptist was a prophet (Matt. 11:9), and in the prophecies of the biblical prophets, unquenchable fire is fire that cannot be prevented from completing its mission. This is evident in both Jeremiah and Ezekiel, as it is certain God never intended that the palaces of Jerusalem (Jer. 17:27) or the forest of the South (Ezk. 20:45–48) burn eternally. Basil Atkinson writes,

> The idea of unquenchable fire is taken like so much else in the New Testament from the Scriptures of the Old. In Jeremiah 17:27 we read that the Lord will kindle a fire in the gates of Jerusalem which will devour her palaces and *shall not be quenched*. The king of Babylon was the instrument through whom God fulfilled this threat, and the palaces were devoured. But is the fire burning now? Of course not. [Yet] No one in the world could quench it

*till it had fulfilled the purpose for which it was kindled ...*
Such will be the fire that will burn up the wicked.[12]

To the certainty of the meaning of the term *burn up* and its usage throughout the New Testament, we can add the certainty that the fire will accomplish its job. Moreover, John chose to communicate his warning in practical, real-world terms that people can easily understand and visualize. If you want an illustration of what will happen to the unsaved in the unquenchable flames of hell, burn some chaff. Everyone knows the result. When burned, chaff disappears into smoke.

As you watch the chaff burn up before your eyes, it will be a somber moment. "For I take no pleasure in the death of anyone, declares the Sovereign Lord. Repent and live!" (Ezek. 18:32, NIV).

At the very beginning of Matthew's Gospel, three factors come together in a manner that inescapably communicates annihilation: chaff, *katakaio*, and unquenchable fire. Chaff is readily combustible. Throughout the New Testament, *katakaio* indicates that something is burned to ashes or utterly consumed. Unquenchable fire is unstoppable fire, fire that cannot be prevented from accomplishing its mission. In powerful, graphic imagery, we learn the fate of the impenitent. Grain husks have no chance of surviving indomitable fire. According to John the Baptist, unsaved sinners face utter incineration.

## EBC, NOT ECT

A second look at the key texts on final judgment led me to the conclusion that John 3:16 should be taken at face value. God sent the Son to die on our behalf so that all who put their trust in Him will have eternal life. All who reject God's offer of reconciliation will perish. Their lives will end. Immortality, then, is conditioned upon faith in Christ. This is plainly appropriate, for one cannot reject his or her Creator and expect to have a place in the Creator's eternal universe—hence the term "conditional immortality" or "conditionalism," or perhaps even better, *Eternal by Choice* (EBC).

When God knocks on the door of a sinner's heart, there is a choice to make. Rejecting Christ leads to death; so does indifference to Him. "Believe on the Lord Jesus Christ, and you will be saved" (Acts 16:31) is the message of the New Testament.

## WHAT'S AHEAD

*Eternal by Choice* records my biblical journey to the truth of final judgment. In the next chapter, we'll visit the crime scene in Genesis that put us all in mortal danger. We'll travel back to the era of the church fathers to see the thinking of those most responsible for ECT theology. An overview of today's debate between conditionalists and traditionalists will also be covered. Chapter three will explore Matthew, the most important book of the Bible when it comes to hell. Moral, philosophical, and pragmatic problems with the traditional view of hell that should have served as red flags for evangelicals will be discussed in chapter four. We'll dig into the book of Revelation in chapter five. Discovering the essential identity of the beast and paying attention to context will correct hasty assumptions commonly held by traditionalists. It will also reveal some important prophetic insights typically missed by premillennial traditionalists.

These studies will, I hope, bring an end to the most glaring and destructive theological error in the history of the church, as well as fill hearts with an overwhelming sense of the goodness of God. These benefits are important, but the truth about final judgment is absolutely crucial when it comes to the challenges of fulfilling the Great Commission in our modern secular world. This will be apparent in the final, sixth chapter.

Let's head now to the Garden of Eden.

## CHAPTER TWO

# GENESIS SHOWS THE WAY

My investigation into divine justice began with the opening chapters of Genesis. There we see God creating the universe and fashioning the planet we all live on. The sunlight we enjoy, the water we drink, the animals we play with—all of it comes from God. Everything does. And originally everything was perfect. All that God created was "very good" (Gen. 1:31).

Of all that God made, humanity stood out as special. Adam and Eve were created in God's image. They were given tremendously important responsibilities. They were charged with managing the planet, including the fish of the sea, the birds of the air, and the animals of the land. They were trusted with making decisions and had a partnership with God. For example, God made the birds and animals, and Adam gave each of them a name.

Most amazingly, Adam and Eve enjoyed fellowship with the Creator Himself. Though it's hard to believe sometimes, this is what God desires. "He is the God who longs to fill our lives and our days with the wealth of His presence. A God who cherishes our companionship," writes David Needham in *Close to His Majesty*.[1]

The friendship and closeness that God desires to have with us does not alter the fact that He is in charge of the universe. He established its laws, not only its physical laws but the moral principles to which all are subject. In short, God is not only the Creator; He is also the Ruler of the universe—the King of kings and Lord of lords (1 Tim. 6:13–16). Thus, He informs Adam and Eve of what is allowed and what is not, as well as the penalty for disobedience.

> Then the Lord God commanded the man, "You may freely eat fruit from every tree of the orchard, but you must not eat from the tree of the knowledge of good and evil, for when you eat from it you will surely die." (Gen. 2:16–17, NET)

Only one limitation was placed on Adam: do not eat from a particular tree in Eden. It was not that the fruit was poisonous. The prohibition was a simple but profound test: Would Adam and Eve trust and obey their Creator? Nor was it that death would be immediate. In the Pentateuch, the first five books of the Bible, "you will surely die" is a judicial expression; it is "a pronouncement of a judge on one who has been condemned to die."[2] God was saying that rebellion merits the death penalty. The Hebrew text speaks of the certainty of coming under the sentence of death.[3] On the day or *when* the forbidden fruit is eaten, the transgressor will be guilty, in the courtroom of the Creator, of a crime worthy of death.

As we know all too well, Adam and Eve disobeyed God's command.

> When the woman saw that the tree produced fruit that was good for food, was attractive to the eye, and was desirable for making one wise, *she took some of its fruit and ate it.* She also gave some of it to her husband who was with her, and *he ate it.* (Gen. 3:6, NET)

The parents of the human race sinned, and death has been with us ever since. Historically, there have been two distinct understandings of God's death penalty: the conditional immortality view and the eternal conscious torment view.

## THE CONDITIONAL IMMORTALITY VIEW OF GOD'S DEATH PENALTY

The conditional immortality view says that "life is the Creator's provisional gift to all, which will ultimately be granted forever to the saved and revoked forever from the unsaved."[4] Conditional immortality, then, takes the penalty for sin—death—at face value, namely, the absence or cessation of life.

Whether Hebrew, Greek, or English, the commonly understood definition of death is the termination of life. Absence or cessation of life is also the standard usage of *death* in the New Testament. *Nekros* is consistently translated *dead*. For example: "Now when they had fulfilled all that was written concerning Him [Jesus], they took Him down from the tree and laid Him in a tomb. But God raised Him from the *dead*" (Acts 13:29–30). *Dead* here obviously refers to the lifeless, crucified body of Christ lying in the tomb. Also, in Acts, the sudden death of Sapphira, a woman who lied to God, is recorded: "Then immediately she fell down at his [Peter's] feet and breathed her last. And the young men came in and found her *dead*, and carrying her out, buried her by her husband" (Acts 5:10). In Sapphira's body, life was *absent*; it had *ceased*, come to an *end*. Other Greek words for death have this same meaning.[5]

If the conditional immortality understanding of God's justice had been fully executed when Adam and Eve sinned, the human race would have ended in Eden, yet Adam and Eve lived for a long time and their family grew larger and larger. Why? Rather than terminating Adam and Eve's lives, God acted in grace because He had a plan for their redemption that would send His Son to Calvary to die for the sins of the whole world (1 Jn. 2:2). Those that receive God's gift of salvation have their sins forgiven (Eph. 1:7) and become members of His forever family (Jn. 1:12). But what if one rejects God's offer of reconciliation?

If one refuses the grace of God, he or she will have no protection from the Genesis 2:17 death penalty. Sinners without a Savior will face final judgment and be cast into the lake of fire (Matt. 25:31–46; Rev. 20:11–15), where both body and soul will be killed, put to death (Matt. 10:28). Explicitly, the unrepentant will burn up in God's judgment fire (Matt. 3:12; 13:30, 40). To quote Peter, when God turned "the cities of Sodom and Gomorrah to ashes he condemned them to extinction, making them an example of what is going to happen to the ungodly" (2 Pet. 2:6, ESV). As Ignatius (A.D. 50–116) succinctly states, "For were He to reward us according to our works, we should cease to be."[6]

*Important Notes*

Christ's crucifixion was an extremely painful death. Similarly, conditionalists believe that there will be anguish and pain in conjunction with the final judgment of unbelievers. It is evident from Jesus' teaching that there will be wailing and gnashing of teeth when sinners are cast into the lake of fire (Matt. 13:50). The extent of the sinner's suffering will be appropriately determined by God, who is both righteous and merciful.

Conditional immortality (also known as CI or conditionalism) held by an ever-growing number of evangelical Christians, affirms that the final judgment has three basic components: a trial before God, suffering, and the irreversible cessation of life. Other terms sometimes used to communicate this same meaning are annihilationism and terminal punishment. Throughout this book, I use the terms *annihilationism*, *conditionalism*, and *terminal punishment* interchangeably.

## TERMINAL PUNISHMENT MAKES GOOD SENSE

The rationale for terminal punishment is straightforward: To reject the Creator is to forfeit the privilege of living in His universe. This penalty is just and understandable. It is unreasonable to expect God to sustain those who spurn Him. The sinner who turns his back on the Creator simply has no right to live in the Creator's universe. In Romans, Paul affirms that death is God's righteous penalty for sin and assures us that even the ancient idol worshippers were not ignorant of heaven's justice:

> For since the creation of the world His invisible attributes are clearly seen, being understood by the things that are made, even His eternal power and Godhead, so that they are without excuse, because, although they knew God, they did not glorify Him as God, nor were thankful, but became futile in their thoughts … and worshiped and served the creature rather than the Creator … who, knowing the *righteous judgment of God*, that those who practice such things are *deserving of death*, not only do the same but also approve of those who practice them. (Rom. 1:20–21, 25, 32)

The ancient idol worshippers knew the righteous judgment of God. They knew they *deserved* to *die* because of the things they were doing. The rationale for the conditional immortality view, then, is not only a matter of common sense but an understanding that dates back to the beginning of human history. Further, CI sets forth a *righteous* penalty, one that is truly deserved.

## THE TRADITIONAL VIEW OF GOD'S DEATH PENALTY

The ECT view says that the unsaved will suffer in hell forever. It is often called *traditionalism* because ECT has been the dominant view of hell for the past 1500 years of church history. Traditionalists also say that death is the penalty for sin. Henry Thiessen writes, "It takes only one word to state the penalty of sin, and thus it is given in the Scriptures, death."[7]

For the traditionalist, however, death means separation from God. Thus, eternal death, as defined by the traditionalist, equals eternal separation from God and involves continual conscious suffering in the lake of fire. Robert Peterson writes,

> Jesus paints a picture of inextinguishable hellfire to depict unbearable and enduring pain. We have all had the experience of being burned. Jesus and his apostles use this common experience to warn their hearers of a far worse fate."[8]

There are, however, a growing number of modern-day traditionalists who affirm eternal separation from God but distance themselves from a hell of wrath and flames of fire. It's increasingly popular to reduce God's role to that of a bystander. *The impenitent want to be free from God, and God grants their wish; sinners go to hell because they want it and choose it,* say many well-known Christian pastors and teachers. This approach seeks a more reasonable traditionalist version of hell but does not achieve it. There are things that just can't be gotten around.

No sinner asked to be born, none of us decreed the penalty for sin, and no one desires endless misery. Whatever the nature of hell, the buck must stop with God, for though we sin of our own free will, the consequence of impenitence is the Creator's prerogative to determine. Moreover, separation from the goodness of God is inherently a nightmare beyond comprehension. Traditionalist Sean McDowell, to his credit, is very honest about what being eternally separated from the goodness of God would mean.

> Try to imagine a place away from the God of relationships. A place without him is a place without relationships, without love, without joy, peace, beauty, satisfaction, contentment, acceptance, affection, fulfillment, laughter, and everything else that is called good. That would be hell—literally. A place void of all that God is would be a place of eternal aloneness—a place called hell…. It is hard to imagine the anguish of such a place—the absolute aloneness of the living dead.[9]

No matter how it is packaged, eternal separation from God equals the endless suffering of mothers and fathers and sons and daughters.

## DEATH IS SEPARATION – A MISNOMER

In evangelical circles, discussion of final judgment typically begins with the statement "death is separation." This has been repeated to the point that "death is separation" is commonly believed to be the biblical definition of death. It is not. It is a theological definition crafted by proponents of ECT in support of their view.

Later in this chapter, we'll discuss how Greek philosophy led to the *death is separation* understanding of final judgment. The traditionalist repeatedly reminds us of his theological definition of death because our minds naturally gravitate to its commonsense literal meaning: the absence of life. Even James 2:26, "For as the body without the spirit is dead, so faith without works is dead also," is based on the fact that death is the absence of life. A dead body neither speaks nor moves nor acts; similarly, faith with neither confession nor praise nor deeds that honor God is dead.

How should the present separation between God and the unsaved be viewed? It is the result of the collision between sin and grace in Eden. Through rebellion sinners became estranged from God. God's grace affords human beings the opportunity to be reconciled to Himself. In light of this, separation between God and the unsaved is simply inescapable, but this situation is temporary. Ultimately, the opportunity to accept grace will end, and the Day of Judgment will come.

Discussion of final judgment ought to begin with the warning that people are in danger of perishing, forever. This crucial message doesn't reach the world when Christians portray death as eternal existence separated from God.

## IT SHOULD BE CALLED ETERNAL *PARTIAL* SEPARATION FROM GOD

Traditionalists should refer to their view as the eternal *partial* separation from God view because it is a partial separation that they propose. No one exists without the sustaining power of God, neither now nor in the future.

God is not only the Creator of the universe but its Sustainer as well. Speaking of the eternal Son of God, Paul writes, "all things were created through him and for him ... and all things are *held together* in him" (Col. 1:16–17, NET). The writer of Hebrews says of the Son, "he *sustains* all things by his powerful word" (Heb. 1:3, NET).

If the partial separation view were true, it's likely God's sustaining power would involve more than holding molecules together. Think about the mental aspect of an eternity in hell with me for a moment. Let's start with a traditionalist description of hell based on the story of the rich man and Lazarus.

> Jesus taught that an unbridgeable chasm separates the wicked in Hell from the righteous in paradise. The wicked suffer terribly, remain conscious, retain their desires and memories, long for relief, cannot find comfort, cannot leave their torment, and have no hope (see Luke 16:19–31).[10]

The rich man was in torment, yet he conversed with Abraham and expressed concern for his brothers. That is, he seemed to be functioning normally. *How would this be possible throughout eternity in hell?* We can take pain and agony for a while, but eternally? Sooner or later, wouldn't unending suffering essentially turn hell into an enormous hospital with two wings: the intensive care unit and the psychiatric ward? How can an eternity of hopelessness not cause the psychological breakdown of the sinner? For the traditionalist understanding to be true, wouldn't God have to be constantly healing and strengthening the mental health of those in hell even as He punishes them and sustains their misery?

But whatever the involvement, whatever the level of assistance, the question is why? *Why would a holy God eternally sustain rebellion and sinfulness that He abhors?* It doesn't make sense that God would, but this is what traditionalism says He does.

## The Irony of the Eternal Separation from God View

If eternal separation from God is the penalty for sin, wouldn't you expect that separation to be true total separation? Herein is a profound irony: *To be totally separated from God is to cease to exist*. It could not be otherwise, for everyone's existence is dependent on the Sustainer.

What view actually holds to total separation? Yes, it is conditionalism that affirms complete separation from God in the second death.

## THE NEED FOR INTEGRITY IN LANGUAGE

We live in a day when language is being terribly abused, especially for political and social engineering purposes. If we're concerned about the rise of Orwellian doublethink in America, should we not be diligent to avoid it ourselves?[11]

Since my days at Multnomah, I've said that salvation is best understood by taking John 3:16 at face value. But, as a traditionalist, I was blind to my own failure to do so when it came to the words *should not perish*. I read *perish* but thought *eternally suffer torment*. This was such an automatic practice that it never occurred to me that I might be reading theology into the text rather than coming to it as a learner. It also never occurred to me that I was guilty of doublethink, but I was. To equate perish with eternal conscious suffering is a blatant contradiction. Like "war is peace," *death is living somewhere forever* is another example of doublethink.

R. F. Weymouth (1822–1902), who produced *The Resultant Greek Testament*, from which came the *Weymouth New Testament* (WNT), died long before George Orwell wrote *1984*, but he recognized doublethink at work in traditionalist theology.

> My mind fails to conceive a grosser misinterpretation of language than when the five or six strongest words which the Greek tongue possesses, signifying "destroy," or "destruction," are explained to mean maintaining an everlasting but wretched existence. To translate black as white is nothing to this.[12]

If ECT were God's truth, there would be no need to turn the meaning of words upside down. Conditionalism, by contrast, takes scripture at face value. Let's open our Bibles to Genesis 2–3 and see which view fits the biblical narrative and which does not.

## WERE ADAM AND EVE TRADITIONALISTS?

Are endless separation from God and eternal torment consistent with the first pages of the Bible, or does the traditionalist understanding of God's death penalty seem out of place in Genesis?

Would Adam and Eve recognize the traditional view of hell, or would the thought of their unsaved grandchildren suffering endlessly come as a shock?

The essence of traditionalism is that every human being exists eternally either in God's presence or separated from Him.

Did Adam hear God say, "If you eat of the tree of the knowledge of good and evil, you will live forever, but you will do so without the benefit of My fellowship"? Did Eve understand God to have said, "If you eat the forbidden fruit, you will exist endlessly on this planet, but never again will I meet with you"?

The traditional view of hell explicitly holds that the penalty for sin is to eternally suffer torment in the lake of fire.

Did God say to Adam in the Garden of Eden, "Adam, if you eat from the tree of the knowledge of good and evil, you will experience pain and suffering that will never end"? An unbiased reading of Genesis chapter 2 could never lead to this conclusion. Nothing in Genesis 2 even hints of eternal torment. "Then the Lord God commanded the man, 'You may freely eat fruit from every tree of the orchard, but you must not eat from the tree of the knowledge of good and evil, for when you eat from it you *will surely die*'" (Gen. 2:16–17, NET).

## ECT'S FAIR-WARNING PROBLEM

The difference between "will surely *die*" and "will suffer *endless torment*" is immense, yet under traditionalism, the two phrases are synonymous. The traditionalist attempt to reconcile this glaring contradiction appeals to the progressive nature of God's revelation and argues that the full implication of death in Genesis 2:17 is revealed in the New Testament. In Adam and Eve's case, however, the penalty for sin was essential information. It defined the peril they faced. If the horror of unending torment was a possibility, shouldn't they have been made aware of this?

Eat from a certain tree in the Garden and you will suffer without relief, eternally. If the traditionalist view is correct, *was Eden a paradise or an immensely frightening danger zone?* ECT is not just another doctrine. If true, it represents a danger a million times worse than the most painful death imaginable. Is it conceivable that God would fail to warn Adam and Eve of such danger?

The traditionalist seeks refuge in progressive revelation because his view cannot be established from the pages of the Old Testament, but progressive revelation provides no satisfactory shelter from the need for fair warning. The earliest scripture typically cited by traditionalists in support of their position is Isaiah 66:24; therefore, for more than half of human history, according to traditionalism, God kept silent about the horrendous danger that loomed over one generation after the next. This is a huge moral problem for traditionalists because providing warning is a biblical principle that God takes very seriously. For example, in Ezekiel, if someone dies because the watchman failed to warn the people of an attack, God "will hold the watchman accountable for that person's death" (Ezek. 33:6, NET).

Furthermore, while revelation is progressive, it is not contradictory. Indeed, God's integrity assures us that the penalty promised in Genesis and the penalty executed in the final judgment will be one and the same. Pause and think about this for a moment.

Suppose a young girl's parents told her that she would lose her allowance for the week if she ate a piece of the apple pie they were saving for a special occasion. But after sneaking a piece of the pie, the girl found herself grounded, confined to her home, until she was eighteen. Feeling indignation at the thought of such parents? Well, if it would be unjust for parents to drastically increase the stated punishment, would it not also be unjust of God to do so?

Paul affirms that the wages of sin is death and assures us that this has always been God's righteous judgment. In Romans 1, Paul takes us back to the creation of the world and the days of Adam, who lived for nearly a millennium. From the beginning, people knew God through the things that He made, but many did not glorify Him as God. Many of Adam's descendants became idol worshippers who knew that they were "deserving of death" (Rom. 1:32) because of their sinful ways.

## IN THE BEGINNING, MAN WAS NOT IMMORTAL

> Then the Lord God said, "Behold, the man has become like one of Us, to know good and evil. And now, *lest he put out his hand* and *take also of the tree of life, and eat,* and *live forever*"— therefore the Lord God sent him out of the garden of Eden to till the ground from which he was taken. (Genesis 3:22–23)

### *Eat and Live Forever*

In light of the widespread assumption that Adam and Eve were created as eternal beings, it's easy to breeze over Genesis 3:22–23, but a closer look reveals that living forever depended upon eating of the tree of life. Traditionalist theologian Millard Erickson acknowledged this when he wrote,

> He [Adam] was not inherently able to live forever, but he need not have died. Given the right conditions, he could have lived on forever.... The impression is given that Adam, even after the fall, could have lived forever if he had eaten

> the fruit of the tree of life. What happened at the time of his expulsion from Eden was that man, who formerly could have either lived forever or died, was now separated from those conditions which made eternal life possible, and thus it became inevitable that he die.[13]

God created Adam and Eve with the intention that they would spend eternity in glorious friendship with Himself, but He did not create them with immortal bodies and souls because true friendship is a mutual decision. To gain eternal life requires that we accept the friendship offered to us by God. This is accomplished through faith. "'Abraham believed God, and it was counted to him as righteousness'—and he was called a friend of God" (Jam. 2:23, ESV).

Scripture teaches that living forever is a blessing God bestows on the basis of faith (Jn. 3:16; Rom. 6:23; 1 Jn. 5:11–13). As the *Pictorial Encyclopedia of the Bible* states, immortality is "not a universal natural possession but the gift of redemptive grace."[14] We are eternal by choice, the choice of trusting in Christ.

## The Survival of the Soul When the Body Dies

If the soul isn't naturally or by creation immortal, why does it survive the death of the body? This is a fair question asked by many. Let's consider it, beginning with the believer's departure to be with Christ.

In his letter to the Philippians, Paul plainly teaches that at death he will depart from his body to be with Christ: "If I am to go on living in the body, this will mean fruitful labor for me.... I desire to depart and be with Christ, which is better by far; but it is more necessary for you that I remain in the body" (1:22–24, NIV). This comforting truth provides no evidence that Adam was created with an immortal soul, however. Through faith in Christ, Paul had become a new creation (2 Cor. 5:17). Paul was in Christ, and Christ was in Paul (Jn. 14:20). The believer's union with Christ (Col. 2:13; 1 Jn. 5:11–12) far exceeds even Adam's pristine pre-fall state of being. It is not by membership in Adam's race but by the Spirit that the believer becomes an eternal being (Jn. 3:5–16), blessed with assurance that to be absent from the body is to be present with the Lord (2 Cor. 4:16–5:8).

As for the unbeliever, it is true that physical death is not the end. There is a very specific reason for this: God has determined that the unsaved sinner will face a final judgment to demonstrate that he or she deserves the lake of fire second death. Prophecy foretells that the departed impenitent will be resurrected to stand before their Maker at the Great White Throne judgment (Jn. 5:28–29; Rev. 20:11–13). It is the *time gap* between physical death and final judgment that accounts for the unbeliever's survival beyond biological death. The unsaved must appear in God's courtroom; therefore, their existence is maintained by God for the Day of Judgment. The fact that God preserves the unsaved for final judgment does not tell us what happens to the impenitent in the lake of fire. This we must learn from the scriptures that declare the destiny of the unsaved.

*Who We Are, Body and Soul*

God made us body and soul (or soul/spirit) united. We are not one or the other but both together. This is the story of Genesis. "The Lord God formed the man from the soil of the ground and breathed into his nostrils the breath of life, and the man became a living being" (Gen. 2:7, NET). The opposing viewpoints—the Platonic "we're a soul that inhabits a body" and the materialist "we're a collection of cells that think"—both miss the mark. Plato greatly undervalued the body. Materialism says that there is nothing more to us than a body. If we're honest about it, we don't presently understand the incredible union of body and soul as we one day will. What is certain is that as we were created body and soul, it is body and soul united, the complete person, that will either live forever in the new earth or be justly terminated.

## PLATO, AUGUSTINE, THE IMMORTALITY OF THE SOUL, AND DEATH IS SEPARATION

The role played by the Greek philosopher Plato (429–347 B.C.) and his belief in the "immortality of the soul" in the development of ECT doctrine can hardly be overstated. Plato's teaching that the soul is inherently eternal (has always existed and will always exist) was widely popular during the early centuries of the church. Thus, many who came to faith in Christ at that time grew up immersed in Platonic tradition. These early Christians rejected Plato's teaching of the preexistence of the soul. Rather, they insisted, the soul had a beginning—after all, God created Adam and Eve—

but it was common for them to agree with Plato that the soul is immortal. This was certainly true of Augustine of Hippo (A.D. 354–430).

Augustine, a Platonist prior to his conversion to Christianity, set forth the traditionalist case for hell in *The City of God*. The connection between the immortality of the soul and Augustine's doctrine of eternal conscious suffering is not veiled:

> As the soul has been *created immortal*, and therefore, although by sin it may be said to die … yet it does not cease living a kind of life, though a miserable [one], because it is *immortal by creation*.[15]

> For the *spirit*, whose presence animates and rules the body, can both suffer pain and *cannot die*. Here then is something which, though it can feel pain, is *immortal*. And this capacity, which we now see in the spirit of all, shall be hereafter in the bodies of the damned.[16]

Despite traditionalist protests that their view of hell was not historically driven by Greek philosophy, the prominence of the immortality of the soul in Augustine's teaching, as in Tertullian's before him,[17] is there for all to see. The fact that traditionalism began on a faulty premise doesn't mean that it can't be true, but it certainly doesn't inspire confidence—neither does Augustine's understanding of eternal death.

> In the last damnation, though man *does not cease to feel*, yet because this feeling of his is neither sweet with pleasure nor wholesome with repose, but painfully penal, it is not without reason called *death* rather than life.[18]

The traditionalist definition of death as separation from God is not only a theological definition, it is a theological definition historically formed in conjunction with the immortality of the soul. Augustine argued that physical death occurs when the immortal soul separates from the mortal body; the soul, being immortal, dies in the sense that God forsakes it or separates His presence from it. Unless rectified by grace, this condition continues as everlasting punishment.[19] This is the thinking from which traditionalism sprang.

Augustine must have been aware that he was redefining death, for he says that in the world to come there will be "death such as now there is not."[20] Death as experienced in our world is the cessation of life, but in the future, according to Augustine, death is living a miserable, God-forsaken life forever. Sound contrived? Philip Hughes comments,

> There is no more radical antithesis than that between life and death, for life is the absence of death and death is the absence of life. Confronted with this antithesis, the position of Augustine cannot avoid involvement in the use of contradictory concepts, for the notion of death that is everlastingly endured requires the postulation that the damned be kept endlessly alive to endure it.... It would be hard to imagine a concept more confusing than that of death, which means existing endlessly without the power of dying. This, however, is the corner into which Augustine (in company with many others) argued himself.[21]

In light of Augustine's belief that everyone lives somewhere forever, one can't help but wonder why he spoke of death at all? But given the Bible's repeated declaration that death is the penalty for sin, Augustine had two choices: rethink his view or live with its contradictions. In spite of this, the assumption that everyone lives somewhere forever continues to be the key principle that sustains ECT theology.

## THE IMMORTALITY CARD STILL IN PLAY

Augustine's conflation of Plato's belief in the soul's innate immortality with the creation of man by God ultimately led to a modified version of Greek philosophy becoming entrenched in the Christian community. Augustine's view was adopted by the Roman Catholic Church and was enshrined in the 1646 *Westminster Confession of Faith*, which states that God "created man, male and female, with reasonable and immortal souls."[22] To this day, belief in the innate immortality of the soul continues to bolster the traditional view of hell.

The common thinking when it comes to the traditional doctrine of hell seems to be this: The idea of eternal conscious suffering is disturbing, but if the human soul is inherently immortal, what other end could there be for those who choose to reject God's salvation? Clark Pinnock writes,

> If souls are immortal, then either all souls will be saved (which is unscriptural universalism) or else hell must be everlasting torment. There is no other possibility since annihilation is ruled out from the start. This is how the traditional view of hell got constructed: add a belief in divine judgment after death (scriptural) to a belief in the immortality of the soul (unscriptural), and you have Augustine's terrible doctrine.[23]

Recognizing that immortality is a gift to be received rather than an inherent aspect of humanity allows for a more clear-minded study of final judgment. It should also be noted that while belief in the immortality of the soul *typically* leads to the conclusion that everyone must live somewhere forever, this overlooks the fact that all of creation is ever dependent on God for existence. Even if "the immortality of the soul" originated in scripture rather than Greek philosophy, the soul would not be beyond God's power to annihilate. Whatever God creates He can destroy.

## IN THE BEGINNING, GOD GUARDED THE TREE OF LIFE

> So He drove out the man; and He placed cherubim
> at the east of the garden of Eden, and a flaming
> sword which turned every way, to guard the
> way to the tree of life. (Genesis 3:24)

Integral to the eternal-torment view is the principle that unbelievers continue endlessly in a sinful state. Genesis 3:24 tells a different story.

### Endless Existence in a Sinful State – Prevented by God

The tree of life was planted in the Garden of Eden (Gen. 2:9) for Adam and Eve to eat freely thereof (Gen. 2:16) and live forever (Gen. 3:22), but after they sinned, God acted decisively to keep humanity away from the tree of life. Why? What did God guarantee by placing mighty cherubim and a flaming sword in Eden? The cherubim and flaming sword ensured that fallen people could not gain access to the fruit that produces immortality. This dramatic move on God's part appears to be in direct conflict with the eternal-torment view.

The traditional view of hell maintains that to reject Christ is to exist throughout eternity as a sinner. Genesis 3:24 reveals that God has taken extraordinary measures to prevent the horrible possibility of human beings continuing forever in a sinful state. The picture of cherubim and a flaming sword guarding the tree of life should serve as a wake-up call to traditionalists everywhere. God in His providence prevents unredeemed sinners from living forever because He is loving and just.

People who never asked to be born are brought into existence by God, given free will, and asked if they will accept their Creator, the blessings of His friendship, and life in His righteous universe. To force people who reject God's gracious offer to remain in His universe would be morally wrong; the appropriate course of action would be to return them to nonexistence. To condemn them to an intolerable eternity of meaninglessness and futility for their honest personal response would be vengeful, unloving, and utterly immoral.

God is glorified when He rescues and redeems people, but there is nothing glorious about unrepentant sinners living forever. The traditional view of hell is inconsistent with the character of God and contrary to His eternal purpose that there will be "new heavens and a new earth in which righteousness dwells" (2 Pet. 3:13). God did not allow sin to enter the human race so that sinners might continue forever;

it is only the redeemed that will live forever: "For all that is in the world—the lust of the flesh, the lust of the eyes, and the pride of life—is not of the Father but is of the world. And the world is passing away, and the lust of it; but he who does the will of God abides forever" (1 Jn. 2:16–17).

Most people, believers or not, accept the need for justice to rectify sinful actions, but finite sins committed by finite people do not warrant infinite suffering. No one wants to see mothers and fathers and sons and daughters suffer forever, especially not the God who placed cherubim and a flaming sword in Eden to keep the unredeemed away from the tree of life.

Cherubim and a flaming sword guarding the tree of life make a striking picture. This scene in Eden brings to mind other Old Testament texts that indicate that the ungodly will not exist forever. Contrasting the righteous and the wicked, the Psalmist declares,

> For yet a little while and the wicked shall be no more;
> Indeed, you will look carefully for his place,
> But it shall be no more.
> But the meek shall inherit the earth,
> And shall delight themselves in the
> abundance of peace. (Ps. 37:10–11)

> The Lord knows the days of the upright,
> And their inheritance shall be forever.
> They shall not be ashamed in the evil time,
> And in the days of famine they shall be satisfied.
> But the wicked shall perish;
> And the enemies of the Lord,

Like the splendor of the meadows, shall vanish.
Into smoke they shall vanish away. (Ps. 37:18–20)

## A DOOR OPENS

When I reread the Genesis account of original sin, eternal torment was conspicuous only by its absence. That Adam and Eve were not created as eternal beings was undeniable. It also struck me that God had decisively acted to prevent people from living forever as sinners. Suddenly the traditional view of hell that I had held for over thirty years seemed out of sync with scripture. Freed from the assumption that eternal torment was a fact, I pressed on with my investigation, full of wonder as to what I might find.

# MATTHEW: THE FOUNDATIONAL BOOK ON HELL

*N*eed some wisdom? Try Proverbs. Want to understand justification by faith? Study Romans and Galatians. Concerned about the fate of unbelievers? More than half of the references to *Gehenna*, the Greek word for hell, are found in Matthew's Gospel. *Gehenna* is derived from the Hebrew *Ge-Hinnom* (Valley of Hinnom), a valley south of Jerusalem.[1] It was in this valley that King Ahaz, who ruled Judah in the eighth century B.C., made horrific child sacrifices (2 Chr. 28:3). Infamous for death by fire, *Gehenna* represents the final judgment fire, the lake of fire (Rev. 20:11–15). On this point conditionalists and traditionalists readily agree.[2]

Matthew also contains a number of passages that refer to final judgment even though they do not use the word *Gehenna*, including Matthew 25:41–46, which is widely acknowledged by traditionalists as the most important passage in the Bible concerning final destinies. The total number of passages in Matthew about hell is impressive, surpassing what any other book has to offer, making Matthew the Bible's primary book on final judgment.

Is hell a place of perishing or eternal torment? In Matthew, we'll learn what Jesus saves us from and hear the warning of coming judgment that He wants Christians to take to the world.

## WHAT TRADITIONALISM GOT RIGHT

Jesus repeatedly affirms the reality of hell and warns us that it is most certainly a place to avoid. To its credit, traditionalism has recognized and faithfully preserved this truth. Traditionalists are also correct when they say that the unsaved will face a final judgment before God, will be cast into the lake of fire, and will suffer an eternal punishment there. The critical issue, however, is what ultimately happens to the impenitent in the lake of fire. What did Jesus mean when He spoke of eternal punishment? We got a preview of Jesus' teaching when we considered the testimony of John the Baptist in chapter one.

Recall that John brought three factors together in Matthew 3:12 that clearly communicate annihilation: chaff, *katakaio*, and unquenchable fire. Chaff is readily combustible. Throughout the New Testament, *katakaio* indicates that something is burned to ashes or utterly consumed. Unquenchable fire is unstoppable fire, fire that cannot be prevented from accomplishing its mission. In powerful, graphic imagery, John tells us that unsaved sinners face utter incineration. As we consider the words of Jesus in Matthew's Gospel, nothing will contradict the testimony of John and much will confirm it.

## THE SERMON ON THE MOUNT WARNINGS

The first warning in the Sermon on the Mount is very brief. Jesus speaks of the "danger of hell fire" (Matt. 5:22), but He does not tell us anything more. It is what I call a generic warning, one that affirms hell's reality but does not disclose what happens there. The next warnings in the Sermon on the Mount are somewhat more detailed.

> If your right eye causes you to sin, tear it out and throw it away. For it is better that you lose one of your members than that your whole body be thrown into hell. And if your right hand causes you to sin, cut it off and throw it away. For it is better that you lose one of your members than that your whole body go into hell. (Matthew 5:29–30, ESV)

Contrasting a part with the whole, Jesus says that it is better to lose a member of one's body, such as an eye or a hand, than to have one's whole body cast into *Gehenna*. Does Jesus say this because the lake of fire is a place of eternal torment, or is it that the lake of fire burns up those cast into it? These are generic warnings that do not specifically tell us what happens in hell.

### *The Broad Way Warning*

> Enter by the narrow gate; for wide is the gate and
> broad is the way that leads to *destruction* [*apoleia*],

> and there are many who go in by it. Because narrow
> is the gate and difficult is the way which leads to *life*,
> and there are few who find it. (Matthew 7:13–14)

*Destruction* in Matthew 7:13 is contrasted with *life* in Matthew 7:14. The opposite of life is *death*, a basic meaning of *apoleia*. For example, in Acts, Jewish religious authorities thought Paul was unfit to live and wanted Roman officials to have him executed. Festus, Roman procurator of Judea, responded, "It is not the custom of the Romans to deliver any man to destruction (*apoleia*) before the accused meets the accusers face to face, and has opportunity to answer for himself concerning the charge against him" (Acts 25:16).

Traditionalists make much of the fact that Jesus talked about hell more than any of the writers of the New Testament, but what did Jesus actually say about hell? If the broad way leads to ECT, why didn't Jesus plainly say so? He surely couldn't be embarrassed or afraid to declare His sovereignly chosen penalty for sin, could He? Jesus states in Matthew 7:13 that destruction, being put to death, is the end of the unsaved.

## OUTER DARKNESS

When we think of hell, fire immediately comes to mind, but Jesus also spoke of outer darkness (Matt. 8:12, 22:13, 25:30). The distinction between fire and darkness may indicate that both are figurative with regard to final judgment. It may be, however, that the fire is literal and the darkness figurative of death. Not only is fire the more dominant reference, but fire is the means by which the present universe will come to an end (2 Pet. 3:10–13).

Whether fire and/or darkness are figurative is debatable, but either way the final result is the same. If outer darkness speaks of final judgment, as most traditionalists and conditionalists believe, then it must represent the same ultimate reality as final judgment fire. Since the chaff (unsaved) are utterly incinerated in final judgment fire, final judgment darkness must also indicate cessation of life. Let's take a look at Jesus' first mention of outer darkness.

> Assuredly, I say to you, I have not found such great faith, not even in Israel! And I say to you that many will come from east and west, and sit down with Abraham, Isaac, and Jacob in the kingdom of heaven. But the sons of the kingdom will be cast out into outer darkness. There will be weeping and gnashing of teeth. (Matt. 8:10–12)

These words of Jesus followed His encounter with a Roman military officer, a man who demonstrated great faith in Jesus. Speaking to a Jewish audience at Capernaum, Jesus emphasizes that faith, not nationality, is essential to having a part in God's kingdom. Without faith, even the descendants of Abraham, Isaac, and Jacob will be barred from the kingdom and cast into outer darkness.

Scripture uses darkness and blackness to speak of non-existence. When Job cursed the day of his birth, wishing that it could be obliterated, he said: "May that day be darkness" (Job 3:4); "May darkness and black doom claim it" (Job 3:5, NASB); "That night—may thick darkness seize it; may it not be included among the days of the year nor be entered in any of the months" (Job 3:6, NIV).

Peter seems to be referring to outer darkness when he says that the "blackness of darkness" is reserved for false teachers (2 Pet. 2:17). In this same chapter, Peter declares that God's turning the cities of Sodom and Gomorrah into ashes serves as "an example of what is coming for the ungodly" (2 Pet. 2:6, NASB). Jude also says that "the blackness of darkness" (v. 13) is reserved for the ungodly. Like Peter, Jude cites the destruction of Sodom and Gomorrah as an example of divine judgment (v. 7). That Peter and Jude remind their readers of the ashes of Sodom and Gomorrah affirms the conditionalist view.

That the blackness of darkness is a common way of understanding death is something I can personally attest to. One night, when I was about twelve years old, the fear of death gripped me. I shared my fear with my mom. She was sympathetic, but not being born-again at the time, she didn't have any answers other than saying that she was older and wasn't worried about it. I can still remember sensing death as complete darkness, utter nothingness. Similarly, Francis Schaeffer used the image of a "very black blackboard which had never been used"[3] to illustrate nothingness or what he called "*nothing* nothing."[4]

> On this blackboard we drew a circle and inside that circle there was everything that was—and there was nothing within the circle. Then we erase the circle. This is nothing nothing.[5]

Ultimately, we may not be able to know exactly how the original recipients of Matthew's Gospel understood "outer darkness," but surely outer darkness is functionally equal to unquenchable fire in which chaff and tares *burn up*, indicating permanent cessation of life.

## WEEPING AND GNASHING OF TEETH

Weeping and gnashing of teeth is found six times in Matthew. The instance in Matthew 8:10–12 is clarified by a passage in Luke's Gospel. Specifically addressing those who could say, "We ate and drank in Your presence, and You taught in our streets" (Lk. 13:26), Jesus declares: "There will be weeping and gnashing of teeth, when you see Abraham and Isaac and Jacob and all the prophets in the kingdom of God, and yourselves thrust out" (Lk. 13:28). *When you see* what you thought was going to be yours but are denied it, says Jesus, there will be weeping and gnashing (grinding) of teeth.

Jesus' warning to the people of Israel has timeless application. Failure to reach a lifelong goal due to misguided choices can be devastating. We'll talk more about weeping and gnashing of teeth when we come to Matthew 13. Right now, there are two important points to be made: First, nowhere is it said that weeping and gnashing of teeth lasts forever; second, weeping and gnashing of teeth is compatible with terminal punishment. Wailing, fear, anger—what else would be expected from sinners cast into an unquenchable fire that scripture declares will burn them up?

## DEGREES OF SUFFERING

> And whoever will not receive you nor hear your words,
> when you depart from that house or city, shake off the

> dust from your feet. Assuredly, I say to you, it will be
> more tolerable for the land of Sodom and Gomorrah in the
> day of judgment than for that city! (Matthew 10:14–15)

In *Matthew 10:5–15*, Jesus compared first-century Jewish cities with notoriously wicked ancient Gentile cities. Jesus said it will be more tolerable in the Day of Judgment for the Gentile cities than for Jewish cities that reject His apostles. It appears that this is related to the fact that greater works of God took place in the Jewish cities. Sodom had the testimony of Lot, who spoke out against sin (Gen. 19:9), but the apostles' preaching to the cities of Israel was accompanied by healing the sick, cleansing lepers, and casting out demons (Matt. 10:8). Surely the Day of Judgment will be more tolerable for Sodom and Gomorrah in the sense that they did not squander a privilege as great as having witnessed the miracles of Christ's apostles.

This concept is also seen in Matthew 11:20–24 where Jesus says that it will be more tolerable for Tyre, Sidon, and Sodom in the Day of Judgment than for Jewish cities that witnessed His mighty works and yet did not repent. It is one thing to be born into a Gentile culture and fail to humble yourself before God. It's another to be born into the nation of Israel, regularly hear the Word of God publicly declared, have the Messiah Himself come to your town and perform miracles before your eyes, and still not repent. Moreover, the misery of unsaved Israel's judgment is further compounded by the fact that they pursued righteousness but did not attain it because they did not seek it by faith (Rom. 9:31–32).

Traditionalists contend that varying degrees of suffering experienced by sinners in hell argues against conditionalism. "There are no degrees of annihilation," says Alan Gomes, "One is either annihilated or one is not."[6] Gomes' comment ignores the fact that conditionalists also affirm that final judgment involves various degrees of suffering. The question is, does the Bible teach *eternal* degrees of suffering? In my book *Rescue from Death*, I investigated every scripture reference cited by Gomes and discovered that none of the passages that Gomes cites say anything about eternal degrees of suffering.[7] What emerged from that review is that of the two views only conditionalism can successfully account for degrees of suffering in the final judgment.

## *Few Stripes Is Incompatible with Eternal Suffering*

Traditionalists have a huge problem when it comes to degrees of suffering because Jesus not only speaks of many stripes but also of *few* stripes for some unbelievers.

> And that servant who knew his master's will, and did not prepare himself or do according to his will, shall be beaten with many stripes. But he who did not know, yet committed things deserving of stripes, *shall be beaten with few.* (Lk. 12:47–48)

First, when confronted with the reality of unbelievers who are hardworking, community-minded individuals, some traditionalists attempt to soften the blow of hell by pointing out that there will be sinners who are beaten with "few stripes."

This type of thinking is indefensible. Eternal separation from God and His goodness is a nightmare beyond imagination.

Secondly, can anyone explain how a person could exist endlessly in the lake of fire and suffer *few stripes*? If a person received but one stripe in an entire year, a trillion years later, he would have suffered a trillion stripes. In light of eternity, that would be a drop in the bucket of the suffering yet to be experienced. Let's be realistic: few stripes in an eternity of suffering is mathematically impossible and functionally nonsensical. Conditionalism, by contrast, is able to account for *few* and *many* stripes.

Varying degrees of suffering in connection with final judgment will reasonably flow not only from differences in opportunity but also from differences in deeds among unbelievers. This is an important principle because the unsaved who die shortly after reaching the age of accountability with few offences recorded in the books of heaven (Rev. 20:12) deserve a much quicker and far less painful death than those that willfully commit terrible crimes over a long period of time. The amount of suffering a person experiences when being consumed in the lake of fire will be in accordance with what God deems appropriate for each individual.

## THE DECISIVE GEHENNA WARNING

> And do not fear those who kill the body but cannot kill the soul. But rather fear Him who is able to *destroy* [*apolesai*] both soul and body in hell. (Matthew 10:28)

Some twenty years ago, after studying the opening chapters of Genesis, the verse that immediately came to mind was Matthew 10:28; I remembered that Jesus had spoken about soul and body being destroyed in hell, and I sensed that a fresh look at the passage would be critically important. Of all the verses in which the word *Gehenna* is found, Matthew 10:28 is the most specific statement on hell that we have.

### Reading Matthew 10:28 in Context

In Matthew 10, Jesus sent His disciples on a challenging mission to the nation of Israel (vv. 5–6). Jesus warns of the dangers: "Behold, I send you out as sheep in the midst of wolves" (v. 16); "But beware of men, for they will deliver you up to councils and scourge you in their synagogues" (v. 17); "You will be brought before governors and kings for My sake" (v. 18); "Now brother will deliver up brother to death" (v. 21); "And you will be hated by all for My name's sake" (v. 22).

Some will denounce the disciples as evil (v. 25), but in the end, truth will prevail: "there is nothing covered that will not be revealed" (v. 26).

The disciples' mission is to proclaim boldly Christ's message (v. 27). Given the severity of the obstacles they will face—arrests, beatings, hatred—Jesus seeks to strengthen the disciples' resolve by putting the situation in proper perspective. Yes, the disciples will encounter physical dangers, possibly even death, but their adversaries have limited power. They can kill your body, but they cannot kill your soul, says Jesus. Consider these words of our Savior carefully. Pay attention to them because they are the immediate context established by Jesus Himself for this passage. Human authorities have the power to stop your heart from beating, but they cannot kill your soul. They cannot put your entire being to death. Therefore, do not fear them, says Jesus. Rather, fear Him who is able to _ _ _ _ both soul and body in hell.

Given the context, what word would you expect to find in the blank space above? As Jesus prefaces His teaching with the fact that people can kill the body but cannot kill the soul, *kill* is the obvious choice. Fear Him who is able *to kill* both soul and body in hell. Here is power so staggering that it should embolden the disciples to stand up to every human threat. It certainly looks like Jesus warns that the very existence of the impenitent will be terminated in hell.

### *Does Destroy Mean Kill in Matthew 10:28?*

The context calls for it, but does *apolesai* mean kill? Did Jesus actually say that God can kill, put to death, both soul and body in hell? If we're to be instructed by Matthew 10:28, we need to let it speak. Have you ever been so locked into a particular view that you'd hunt for a way to make verses say what your theology needs them to say? I've felt that pressure but not in this instance twenty years ago when I came to Matthew 10:28. I knew the importance of the verse, and all I wanted to do was to take it in without any preconceptions. I hope that's your mindset right now.

In the New Testament, there are five other times *apolesai* is applied to human beings. Let's take a look at each of them to see whether or not *apolesai* means kill.

Now when they had departed, behold, an angel of the Lord appeared to Joseph in a dream, saying, "Arise, take the young Child and His mother, flee to Egypt, and stay there until I bring you word; for Herod will seek the young Child to *destroy* Him." (Matt. 2:13)

The wise men were to locate "He who has been born King of the Jews" (Matt. 2:2) and report His location to Herod (Matt. 2:8), but having been divinely warned in a dream that they should not return to Herod, the wise men departed for their own country (Matt. 2:12). When Herod realized that the wise men weren't coming back, "he sent forth and put to death all the male children who were in Bethlehem and in all its districts, from two years old and under, according to the time which he had determined from the wise men" (Matt. 2:16). Is it not perfectly obvious that Herod sought to *kill* the young Child?

Then Jesus said to them, "I will ask you one thing: Is it lawful on the Sabbath to do good or to do evil, to save life or *to destroy it*?" (Lk. 6:9)

*Young's Literal Translation* translates destroy as *to kill*. The NKJV cites "to kill" as the Majority Text reading. Charles B. Williams' *The New Testament: A Translation in the Language of the People* puts it this way: "Is it right on the sabbath to do people good, or to do them evil, to save life or to take it?" This is similar to another succinct verse with *apolesai* in it, the third one on our list: "There is one Lawgiver, who is able to save and *to destroy*. Who are you to judge another?" (Jam.

4:12). We all know that the divine Lawmaker has the power of life and death. In James 4:12, as with Luke 6:9, when an English translation of the Bible uses a word other than destroy, it typically reads "kill" or "put to death."

The fourth verse is quite interesting. Since it is not as familiar as the story of Herod and the young Child, I'll include more of the passage. As you read it, keep in mind that you're going to hear Jesus use the *exact* same word (*apolesai*) that He does in Matthew 10:28.

> Now it came to pass, when the time had come for Him to be received up, that He steadfastly set His face to go to Jerusalem, and sent messengers before His face. And as they went, they entered a village of the Samaritans, to prepare for Him. But they did not receive Him, because His face was set for the journey to Jerusalem. And when His disciples James and John saw this, they said, "Lord, do You want us to command fire to come down from heaven and consume them, just as Elijah did?" But He turned and rebuked them, and said, "You do not know what manner of spirit you are of. For the Son of Man did not come to *destroy* men's lives but to save them." (Lk. 9:51–56)

After encountering Samaritans who did not receive the Savior, the disciples asked Jesus if they should command fire from heaven to consume the Samaritans, even as Elijah had called down fire from heaven to consume King Ahaziah's soldiers (2 Kin. 1:1–14). Jesus replied that He did not come to *apolesai*; He did not come to kill people or burn them up or consume them by fire. His Second Coming will be with flames of fire

(Isa. 66:15–16), but in His First Advent, Jesus came as a sacrificial lamb to die for the sins of the world.

Did you catch that? Jesus equates *apolesai* with literal consuming fire. Let *that* sink in for a minute as we look at the fifth and final verse.

> And He was teaching daily in the temple. But the chief priests, the scribes, and the leaders of the people sought to *destroy* Him, and were unable to do anything; for all the people were very attentive to hear Him. (Lk. 19:47–48)

Does not virtually everyone agree that the Jewish authorities sought *to kill* Jesus?

### More Evidence

Does *apolesai* mean kill? We can now say unequivocally, emphatically yes! It should now be clear that Jesus taught annihilationism, but let's reinforce our word study even further. The root word from which *apolesai* comes is *apollumi* (sometimes transliterated *apollymi*). If we expand our investigation beyond *apolesai* and look at other forms of *apollumi* in similar contexts (i.e., where an authority acts against those who are guilty of wrongdoing or are perceived to be evil), we again find that "destroy" means to kill, put to death. Here are three examples:

First, "But the chief priests and elders persuaded the multitudes that they should ask for Barabbas and *destroy* Jesus" (Matt. 27:20). The chief priests and elders influenced the masses to have Jesus *put to death*. This is clear from Matthew 27:22: "Pilate said to them, 'What then shall I do with Jesus who is called Christ?' They all said to him, 'Let Him be crucified!'"

Second, "He [Jesus] said to the man, 'Stretch out your hand.' And he stretched it out, and his hand was restored as whole as the other. Then the Pharisees went out and immediately plotted with the Herodians against Him, how they might *destroy* Him" (Mark 3:5–6). I don't know anyone who thinks this verse teaches that the Pharisees plotted to discredit Jesus. The Pharisees plotted to *kill* Christ.

Third, Matthew 22:7 is a particularly relevant verse: "But when the king heard about it, he was furious. And he sent out his armies, *destroyed* those murderers, and burned up their city." In the Parable of the Wedding Feast, Jesus tells of a king who had planned the wedding of his son. The king "sent out his servants to call those who were invited to the wedding" (Matt. 22:3). Some of the invited guests ignored the king's servants, but others "seized his servants, treated them spitefully, and killed them" (Matt. 22:6). This king was furious. His military, says Jesus, destroyed the murderers of his servants and burned up their city. In this context of retribution by a king, *destroyed* plainly means *killed.*

### How Traditionalists Handle Matthew 10:28

It is not unusual for a word to have a variety of meanings. Take the English word *pen*, for example. Most commonly, pen refers to a writing instrument, but it might refer to an animal enclosure or to a female swan. It needs to be kept in mind that each particular meaning is valid only within a properly corresponding context. Suppose you were in a classroom and asked if anyone had a pen that you could use. Would it not be bizarre if someone replied: What type of animal do you need to house?

As with English, a Greek word might have multiple meanings, but it does not follow that you may pick whatever meaning you like when studying a passage of scripture. If you want to know what the Bible actually says, the meaning of the word and its context must match; they must rightly correspond to each other. Kittel's *Theological Dictionary of the New Testament* lists four literal meanings of *apollumi*: to destroy/kill; to suffer loss or lose; to perish; to be lost.[8] To illustrate the importance of matching distinct meanings with their respective contexts, let's pause to recall the story of the woman who had ten silver coins and lost one of them. She gets a lamp out to light up the room and diligently searches for her coin. "And when she has found it, she calls her friends and neighbors together, saying, 'Rejoice with me, for I have found the piece which I *lost!*'" (Lk. 15:9). Lost or missing is a meaning of *apollumi* that is well suited to Jesus' lost coin parable, but imagine if someone tried to apply the most common meaning of *apollumi* in the Gospels—kill/die—to the story of the woman and her coins. That would be absurd. Likewise, words such as lost or missing are foreign to the numerous contexts in which people are killed.

Yet how do traditionalists handle Matthew 10:28? Rather than focusing on the specific word for destroy in Matthew 10:28, traditionalists typically turn to other forms of *apollumi* found in passages that deal with material objects to understand what Jesus says about human beings cast into *Gehenna*.

In *Hell under Fire*, Douglas Moo builds the traditionalist case by citing things such as "wineskins that can no longer function because they have holes in them" (Matt. 9:17) and "a coin that is useless because it is 'lost'" (Lk. 15:9).[9] As these inanimate items continue to exist in a ruined or useless state, the traditionalist reasoning goes, so the unsaved will continue to exist in a ruined condition in hell. This is what traditionalists want us to believe about destroy in Matthew 10:28. Does it seem like traditionalists approach Matthew 10:28 as true Bereans or as those determined to defend a particular theological position?

## The Significance of Matthew 10:28

In Matthew 10:28, there is a comparison between the capabilities of human beings and God. No matter how powerful a person may be, he or she cannot kill the soul. God, by contrast, is able to kill both soul and body. This is not to be taken lightly; it's as serious as it gets. Jesus was strengthening His disciples for a challenging mission with the truth of what is going to happen to the impenitent in hell. This is what makes Matthew 10:28 such a tremendous problem for proponents of ECT. If Jesus says that God can kill soul and body in *Gehenna,* the unsaved person's life would come to an end and traditionalism would be undone. And this is precisely what our investigation has demonstrated.

We know, from our own firsthand examination of the biblical texts, how the particular form of the verb *apollumi* in Matthew 10:28 is used in the New Testament with regard to people. Overwhelmingly, the meaning of *apolesai* is *to kill/*

*put to death*. Other forms of *apollumi*, in contexts where an authority acts against those who have been grievously offensive, also mean *to kill*. Moreover, *to kill* perfectly fits the Matthew 10:28 context. Indeed, the verse is structured in a manner that leads one to expect *apolesai* to mean *to kill*.

Thus, we can say with great confidence, "And do not fear those who kill the body but cannot kill the soul. But rather fear Him who is able *to kill* both soul and body in hell" is the face value reading of Matthew 10:28 that takes *apolesai* in its plain, literal, customary sense.

I would go on to discover other incredible biblical texts that powerfully communicate conditionalism, but Matthew 10:28 was the first verse in the New Testament that I turned to and the one that initially gave me assurance that ECT theology was indeed fallacious.

## THE UNSAVED BURN UP LIKE WEEDS CAST INTO A FURNACE OF FIRE

Let both grow together until the harvest, and at the time of harvest I will say to the reapers, "First gather together *the tares* and bind them in bundles *to burn them*, but gather the wheat into my barn." (Matthew 13:30)

Therefore as the tares are gathered and *burned* in the fire, *so it will be at the end of this age*. The Son of Man will send out His angels, and they will gather out of His kingdom all things that offend, and those who practice lawlessness, and will cast

> them into the furnace of fire. There will be wailing
> and gnashing of teeth. (Matthew 13:40–42)

In this parable, Jesus makes it clear that the wheat (saved) and tares (unsaved) are to "both grow together until the harvest" (Matt. 13:30), that "the harvest is the end of the age" (Matt. 13:39), and that the reaping is done by the angels (Matt. 13:39). Next comes a plain-spoken declaration of annihilationism from Jesus: As tares (weeds) on a farm are gathered and burned up, so it will be for the unsaved (Matt. 13:40–42). This is the same teaching that we found in Matthew 3:12 where the chaff is burned up with unquenchable fire, and in another devastating blow to the traditional view of hell, the word for burn used by Jesus in Mathew 13:30 and 13:40 is *katakaio*.

Traditionalists readily acknowledge that Matthew 13:40–42 is about final judgment in hell. They affirm that the tares will be excluded from the kingdom of God, but once again they fail to pay close attention to *how* that will be accomplished. Like the chaff, tares are eliminated from the kingdom of God by being incinerated in fire.

What becomes of weeds cast into a furnace of fire poses no mystery. The tares *katakaio* in fire. W. E. Vine acknowledges that the Greek "signifies to burn up, burn utterly."[10] Alfred Marshall's interlinear English text translates burned as "are consumed."[11] Only by reading Jesus' words with an everyone-must-live-somewhere-forever mindset could the plain meaning of the text be missed. The tares are destined to disappear into smoke, the very end of the ungodly prophesied by the Psalmist thousands of years ago (Ps. 37:20). The incineration of the tares is Jesus' explanation of hell and the Bible's own commentary on eternal punishment.

## Wailing and Gnashing of Teeth

Jesus' vivid teaching on the fiery destruction of the unsaved includes the statement that there will be "wailing and gnashing of teeth." As noted previously, *weeping and gnashing of teeth* are never said to last eternally. The phrase does drive home, however, the reality that a terrible death awaits those whose names are not written in the Book of Life. Gnashing of teeth reflects stress and/or may indicate anger at God on the part of the sinner (Acts 7:54). Harold E. Guillebaud comments,

> These terrible words [weeping and gnashing of teeth] do make quite clear that the destruction is not immediate, and that the purpose of the fire is not to consume only. But they do not remove the impression of the imagery that the wicked are compared to the worthless weeds which are thrown into the fire to be burned up, and to the worthless fish which are thrown away to be got rid of. Penal suffering comes into the application of the parables, for a death by fire is necessarily a very awful death, but it surely is not the main point, or it could not be so entirely lacking in the imagery of the parables themselves.[12]

As Jesus' crucifixion was neither instantaneous nor without suffering, the death of the impenitent in hell will take as much time and involve as much suffering as the record of one's life requires, but that doesn't change the definition of *katakaio* or the reality that weeds are utterly consumed in fire. Nothing in the imagery of the parable indicates anything other than annihilation, as the missionary and Bible translator Guillebaud correctly points out. Divine justice is ultimately fulfilled in the unquenchable flames of hell as the impenitent, like chaff and tares, burn up in God's furnace of fire. There is no more apt term to describe *such a death* than annihilation.

## THE BAD FISH AREN'T PRESERVED – THEY ARE THROWN AWAY

> Again, the kingdom of heaven is like a dragnet that was cast into the sea and gathered some of every kind, which, when it was full, they drew to shore; and they sat down and gathered the good into vessels, but *threw the bad away*. So it will be at the end of the age. The angels will come forth, separate the wicked from among the just, and *cast them into the furnace of fire*. There will be wailing and gnashing of teeth. (Matthew 13:47–50)

In this graphic warning, the good fish (the saved) are gathered into containers, but the bad (the unsaved) are cast into the furnace of fire. When corrupted things are thrown away into a furnace of blazing flames, is it not expected that the fire will consume what is discarded?

Nebuchadnezzar was astonished to see Shadrach, Meshach, and Abed-Nego unharmed in the midst of the burning fiery furnace (Dan. 3:19–25), and the bush not consumed by fire was a strange sight to Moses (Ex. 3:1–3). Is it not also astonishing and strange that the traditionalist interpretation is exactly opposite to the plain sense of the passage? Under traditionalism, the bad fish are preserved, yet the thought of preserving the bad fish is utterly foreign to the parable. The bad fish are *thrown away*.

The fires of hell are in view yet again in the next warning.

## THE ETERNAL FIRE THAT CONSUMES

> And if your hand or your foot is causing you to sin, cut it off and throw it away from you; it is better for you to enter life maimed or without a foot, than to have two hands or two feet and be thrown into the *eternal fire*. And if your eye is causing you to sin, tear it out and throw it away from you. It is better for you to enter life with one eye, than to have two eyes and be thrown into the *fiery hell*. (Matthew 18:8–9 NASB)

The fires of *Gehenna* are referred to as "eternal fire" in Matthew 18. Traditionalists claim this indicates that the fire's fuel supply—the unsaved—is never consumed. Gomes writes, "the fire of judgment is no normal fire: it is described as an *eternal* fire (Jude 7)."[13] Gomes is right to say that "eternal fire" is unique, but what is the nature of its uniqueness? Gomes claims that the fire does its work "through a process of endless combustion."[14] Was the "eternal fire" of Jude 7 a matter of endless combustion? The answer is simply no.

Jude tells us that Sodom and Gomorrah suffered the punishment of eternal fire. Since these cities were burned to the ground rather quickly by fire that came from the Lord out of the heavens, perhaps eternal fire might best be understood as *divine* fire, the fire of our eternal God. As you read the story of Sodom and Gomorrah, what picture does it leave in your mind?

> The sun had risen on the earth when Lot came to Zoar. Then the Lord rained on Sodom and Gomorrah sulfur and fire from the Lord out of heaven. And he overthrew those cities, and all the valley, and all the inhabitants of the cities, and what grew on the ground.... And Abraham went early in the morning to the place where he had stood before the Lord. And he looked down toward Sodom and Gomorrah and toward all the land of the valley, and he looked and, behold, the smoke of the land went up like the smoke of a furnace. (Gen. 19:23–28, ESV)

The biblical record of Sodom and Gomorrah's judgment does not paint a picture of ongoing torment. Instead, it stuns us with death via catastrophic destruction. As 2 Peter 2:6 states, God "condemned the cities of Sodom and Gomorrah by burning them to ashes, and made them an example of what is going to happen to the ungodly" (NIV).

Truly, the ashes of Sodom and Gomorrah testify to the consuming nature of God's eternal fire (Gen. 19:23–28; 2 Pet. 2:6; Jude 7).

## THE FALLING STONE GRINDS TO POWDER

In Matthew 21, Jesus was welcomed by huge crowds when He came to Jerusalem (vv. 1–11), but the chief priests and the elders of the people confronted Him, demanding to know where He got the authority for His deeds and teachings (v. 23).

Jesus responded with a series of questions and parables, including the parable of the tenant farmers. In this parable, a landowner built a vineyard which he leased to tenant farmers before traveling to a faraway country (v. 33). When the landowner sent his servants to collect his portion of the crop, the tenants beat one servant, killed another, and stoned a third (v. 35). Then the landowner sent his son, saying, "They will respect my son" (v. 37). Maliciously, however, the tenants killed the landowner's son (v. 39).

Having told this story, Jesus asked, "Now when the owner of the vineyard comes, what will he do to those tenants?" (v. 40, NET). Apparently caught up in the story, the Jewish leaders passionately replied: "He will utterly destroy those evil men! Then he will lease the vineyard to other tenants who will give him his portion at the harvest" (v. 41, NET). What Jesus said next identified Israel's faithless leaders as the evil tenants and painted a vivid picture of judgment:

> Have you never read in the Scriptures: "The *stone* which the builders rejected has become the chief cornerstone. This was the Lord's doing, and it is marvelous in our eyes"? Therefore I say to you, the kingdom of God will be taken from you and given to a nation bearing the fruits of it. And whoever falls on this *stone* will be broken; but *on whomever it falls, it will grind him to powder* (vv. 42–44).

Jesus' warning of the stone that grinds to powder brings to mind King Nebuchadnezzar's dream in Daniel chapter two. In his dream, King Nebuchadnezzar saw a dazzling image with a head of gold, chest and arms of silver, belly and thighs of bronze, legs of iron, and feet of iron and clay. Each metal represented a major Gentile kingdom, from Nebuchadnezzar's kingdom (gold), to Medo-Persia (silver), to Greece (bronze), to Rome (iron). Since the metals represent specific kingdoms, iron in the legs and feet suggests that the Roman Empire is in view in both. Clay, in the feet, adds a new element to the image. Thus, many believe that the feet of iron and clay represent an empire that is in some way connected with the historic Roman Empire, yet is also distinct from it. When Christ returns to establish His throne on the earth, He will utterly destroy the kingdoms represented by the image. God gave Nebuchadnezzar a dramatic vision of this:

> You watched while a *stone* was cut out without hands, which *struck the image* on its feet of iron and clay, and broke them in pieces. Then the iron, the clay, the bronze, the silver, and the gold were crushed together, and became like chaff from the summer threshing floors; the wind carried them away so that *no trace of them was found*. And the *stone* that struck the image became a great mountain and filled the whole earth. (Dan. 2:34–35)

First-century Jews longed for the promised Messianic kingdom and deliverance from Roman rule. Israel's rejection of her King, however, would result in the Son's returning to heaven until "they acknowledge their offense" and earnestly seek Him (Hosea 5:15); thus, it would be a future generation of Israelites who would be delivered from a future iron and clay empire. This is the premillennial futurist view. You might have a different end-times perspective, but surely all believers agree that when Jesus comes again the kingdoms of this world will be destroyed so completely that *no trace* of them will remain.

The annihilation of world powers is clearly taught in the Book of Daniel. This in itself does not prove that individual sinners will be annihilated. It is Jesus' application of the annihilation pictured in Daniel to Israel's unbelieving leadership that merits our attention:

> "And whoever falls on this stone will be broken; but *on whomever it falls*, it will *grind him to powder*." Now when the chief priests and Pharisees heard His parables, they perceived that He was speaking of them. (Matt. 21:44–45)

Jesus is the chief cornerstone. He is also the Stone that, in righteous judgment, reduces the condemned to powder. Regardless of one's end-times view, the picture of being ground to powder by the Stone should be clear to all. As the empires of this world will be obliterated at Christ's return, those that reject the Savior will be similarly destroyed. Yet again, Jesus uses stunning annihilation imagery to describe the judgment of unbelievers.

We now have a well-established pattern of teaching. Repeatedly, we have been told what will happen to the impenitent in the final judgment. Because the Bible is self-consistent, we can be confident that other scriptures on hell will prove compatible with the explicit instruction that we have received from Matthew, including the famous judgment of the sheep and the goats.

## THE JUDGMENT OF THE GOATS

> Then He will also say to those on the left hand,
> "Depart from Me, you cursed, into the everlasting fire
> prepared for the devil and his angels." (Matthew 25:41)

Traditionalists argue that since the goats are cast into the same lake of fire as the devil and his angels, they all share the same fate. It is certainly true that unrepentant sinners and Satan share the same fate in the sense that both are cast into the lake of fire. It does not clearly follow that human beings and Satan have the same experience there, however.

First, in Matthew 25:41 we see the goats sent into the lake of fire, but we are not told what happens to them there. Second, with regard to sin, God has dealt distinctly with men and angels. For example, Jesus died for Adam's fallen race, but He did not die for fallen angels (Heb. 2:9, 14–16). In light of this, why should anyone assume that God deals the same with both when it comes to the lake of fire? Third, Satan and the fallen angels (Rev. 12:3–4, 7–9) are significantly more powerful beings than humans are (2 Pet. 2:11). Fourth, fire is not an unfamiliar setting to angelic beings. Consider the vison of cherubim that Ezekiel had when he was by the Chebar River:

> In the midst of the living beings there was something that looked like burning coals of fire, like torches moving among the living beings. The fire was bright, and lightning was flashing from the fire. And the living beings ran back and forth like bolts of lightning.... These are the living beings that I saw beneath the God of Israel by the river Chebar; so I knew that they were cherubim. (Ezk. 1:13–14, 10:20, NASB)

Angelic beings are obviously quite different from human beings. It is noteworthy that Satan was a cherub who "walked back and forth in the midst of fiery stones" (Ezek. 28:14). Because the lake of fire was designed for celestial beings, it should not be assumed that unsaved men and women will have the same experience as Satan in the lake of fire. Destruction is often the result when something is put into an environment for which it was not designed. If fish, for example, are thrown into a desert prepared for snakes, what happens to the fish? Think of how careful you have to be with what goes into a microwave; metal forks can start fires, and some foods will explode.

## The Unequal Yoking of Scripture

Interpreting Matthew 25:41 in light of Revelation 20:10 has long been a key traditionalist practice. Peterson calls Revelation 20:10 "Scripture's own commentary on Matthew 25:41,"[15] but does the suffering of the devil, beast, and false prophet in Revelation 20:10 represent the eternal destiny of the unsaved?

The principle that scripture interprets scripture does not allow us to randomly pair verses. There must be a compelling basis to interpret one passage in light of another. Are human beings the subject of Revelation 20:10? I believe not. When we examine Revelation 20:10 in its own context, I believe we find clear evidence that it is the last verse in a section of scripture dealing with Satan. Do the beast and the false prophet provide a reliable link between Matthew 25:41 and Revelation 20:10?

If the beast and the false prophet are sinners like you and me, it could be argued that they are representative of humanity and foreshadow the fate of unbelievers. In reviewing the book of Revelation, however, I was reminded that the beast and the false prophet are so closely identified with Satan that even traditionalist theologians commonly refer to the devil, the beast, and the false prophet as the satanic trinity. The closer I looked at the details found in Revelation, the more distinct from humankind the beast and false prophet appeared. For example, the beast dies and lives again (Rev. 13:3–14), ascending out of the abyss (Rev. 17:8) that houses fallen angels (Lk. 8:31; Rev. 20:1–3). Also unprecedented are the crimes of the beast and the false prophet. According to Revelation 13:1–17, after being granted authority over every tribe, tongue, and nation, the beast and the false prophet will assault the entire world—small and great, rich and poor, free and slave—with a devastating combination of deceit and coercion designed to force humanity to reject the Creator. *Billions* will be pressured, by the very real threat of death, to worship the beast and take his mark.

To interpret Matthew 25:41 in light of Revelation 20:10 would require rock-solid assurance that the beast and false prophet are intended to be viewed as representative of unsaved sinners in Revelation 20:10, and that is certainly not the case.

## ETERNAL PUNISHMENT

> And these will go away into everlasting punishment,
> but the righteous into eternal life. (Matthew 25:46)

We now come to the verse traditionalists count as the clearest, strongest, and most important affirmation of their view. That a generic warning of hell with very limited detail is the best traditionalism has to offer is quite telling. The danger posed by ECT demands unambiguous, explicit declaration. Matthew 25:46 does not provide that; nevertheless, traditionalists act as if it did. For example, Randy Alcorn cites the dual use of *eternal* in Matthew 25:46 and concludes, "Thus, according to our Lord, if some will consciously experience Heaven forever, then some must consciously experience Hell forever."[16] This conclusion goes beyond the words of the text. Matthew 25:46 does not elaborate on the punishment.

Alcorn asserts that Matthew 25:46 teaches ECT, in part, because he does not see any other viable punishment. Arguing against the doctrine of annihilationism, Alcorn asks, "In what sense does an annihilated person, who by definition experiences nothing, experience any punishment at all?"[17]

At the heart of the "annihilation isn't punishment" argument is the premise that suffering is the only legitimate form of punishment. Gomes writes: "If suffering is lacking, so is punishment."[18] He goes to say: "Punishment demands the existence of the one being punished."[19] Books such as Exodus and Leviticus, however, teach that there is an appropriate penalty for every transgression. In many cases, death is named as the punishment for sin. In fact, death is listed as the penalty for sin multiple times even in a single chapter of scripture (Ex. 21:12, 14, 15, 16, 17, 23, 29).

Government has the power to administer capital punishment, but man can kill only the body. God alone has the power to put to death both soul and body, as we have seen. Rejecting the grace of God will ultimately result in the Genesis 2:17 punishment for sin being carried out. Inasmuch as death is God's ordained penalty for sin (Gen. 2:15–17; Rom. 1:32, 6:23), would not God's termination of soul and body constitute punishment?

When a government carries out the death penalty, we certainly do not conclude that the lawbreaker escaped punishment. Through the death penalty, the government deprives the lawbreaker of the life that he or she might have had in this world. As governments can deny lawbreakers the right to belong to society, God's justice will deny unbelievers the privilege of having a place in His eternal universe and its untold blessings.

## Annihilation Is an Eternal Punishment

The parallel between eternal punishment and eternal life in Matthew 25:46 informs us that the goats experience a punishment in the lake of fire (Matt. 25:41) that is as eternal as the life that the sheep find in Christ's kingdom (Matt. 25:34). Does annihilationism meet this standard? Indeed, it does.

Annihilation as eternal punishment is rooted in the Creator's purpose and program for humankind. The God of everlasting love and goodness created humanity with the intention that we might eternally enjoy His fellowship and immense blessing in a universe in which righteousness dwells; however, God does not force this incredible opportunity on anyone, nor will His holiness allow unredeemed sinners to be part of His forever family. Thus, we find two options placed before people throughout scripture.

In the Garden of Eden were two unique trees: one that led to eternal life and one that led to death. In John 3:16, the believer in Christ shall not perish but have eternal life. The Bible closes with two possible human destinies: the second death and life in the new earth. From cover to cover, God's program is plainly declared: *"I have set before you life and death"* (Deut. 30:19).

To reject the Savior is to face a final death whereby eternal life in the new earth and heaven is irreversibly denied. Conditional immortality takes this death literally. The unsaved will burn up just as surely as do weeds cast into a furnace of fire. This guarantees that each day believers enjoy throughout eternity is a day denied to the unsaved. Under conditionalism, then, the punishment of the unsaved is precisely as long as the life of the redeemed.

Just as capital punishment deprives the executed of all the days that otherwise would have been his or hers, those terminated in hell are deprived of the eternal bliss that could have been theirs. This is not only a punishment that is eternal, it is heartbreaking: the life of somebody's father, somebody's mother, somebody's son, somebody's daughter—gone, forever.

The termination of the sinner in the lake of fire is an eternal death, but is it biblically proper for a one-time event of eternal consequence to be designated as eternal? Indeed, it is. E. Earle Ellis writes,

> When Hebrews speaks of "an everlasting salvation" (σωτηρία αἰωνία, 5:9) or "an everlasting redemption" (αἰωνία λύτρωσις, 9:12) accomplished by the sacrifice of Christ "once for all" (ἐφάπαξ 9:12; cf. 7:27; 10:10), it is clear that it does not mean an everlasting process of saving or redeeming, but rather a one-time act of salvation and redemption that has an everlasting effect.[20]

In light of the biblical precedent for a one-time act of eternal consequence being deemed eternal, there should be no objection to the utter destruction of soul and body being deemed eternal punishment. The fact remains that Matthew 25:46 is too limited in content to clarify the punishment that takes place in the lake of fire. To determine the precise nature of the punishment to which Jesus refers, we need explicit biblical input on the fate of the unsaved in *Gehenna*. Identifying those scriptures is the challenge we face.

## Lessons from My Time at Multnomah

As a young believer studying at the Multnomah School of the Bible in Portland, Oregon, I was privileged to take Bible Study Methods from James Braga. One day, he gave us a passage of scripture and asked that we write down everything that we saw in the text. As we did, he slowly walked up and down the aisles looking at everyone's papers. When he came to my desk, he paused and said, "Look, look again." After this happened a few more times, I couldn't help but wonder if everyone else really had that much more written down. But the lesson stuck with me. Good Bible study is hard work. You've got to look closely at what is and is not actually in the text.

Unfortunately, when it came to hell, this lesson was of little benefit to me for many years because I was not open to truly studying hell. I had compartmentalized it; it was a closed subject. When I finally became a Berean student of the Word, I discovered that traditionalist proof texts never actually say what traditionalists claim they do. If you think you've found a passage of scripture that teaches that human beings are going to consciously suffer forever, I'd say to you, as James Braga said to me, "Look, look again."

Another principle that Braga's class emphasized was the careful study of both the immediate and larger context. When preaching on a passage of scripture, pastors typically bring out details from the immediate context in explaining the text. This is good, but also important is the larger context. Each book of the Bible has a particular purpose and flow of thought. The more we read Paul's letter to the Romans, for example, from beginning to end, the clearer the sections that make up the book become. Reading and rereading an entire book of the Bible prior to digging down into specific verses is a lesson from my days at Multnomah that is especially helpful when considering Matthew 25:46.

### The In-Context Interpretation of Eternal Punishment

Because Matthew 25:46 is of such limited detail, we need unambiguous insight on hell from other texts to clarify exactly what the eternal punishment Jesus speaks of entails. Where should we turn first? Which scriptures deserve our utmost attention? Without a doubt, eternal punishment in Matthew 25:46 is best understood in light of its primary context, Matthew's Gospel.

God gave us the book of Matthew as a basic unit of study. In this Gospel, a number of passages address the final judgment of unbelievers. Would God not expect us to notice these texts and keep them in mind when interpreting the judgment of the goats?

This simple question is so important it needs to be asked again. Do we not have an obligation to understand eternal punishment in light of what God says about final judgment throughout the book of Matthew? We do. Thus, when Jesus tells us that the unsaved will utterly burn up like weeds cast into a furnace of fire and that the Stone will grind the impenitent to powder, we have no right to forget this when we come to 25:41–46. Likewise, when John the Baptist tells us that the chaff, the unsaved, will be incinerated, we must keep this in mind when we see the goats cast into the lake of fire.

Matthew's Gospel is home to the most explicit statements about hell in the Bible. In Matthew, the chaff is incinerated (3:12), broad is the way that leads to destruction in the sense of death (7:13), the killing of soul and body in hell is reason to fear God (10:28), tares are gathered and utterly burned up in fire (13:30, 40), the bad fish are thrown away into a furnace of fire (13:47–50), and the falling Stone grinds to powder (21:44).

Through vivid scenes of utter destruction, scripture seeks our attention and powerfully conveys the seriousness and finality of God's righteous penalty for sin: cessation of life. Thankfully, this does not have to be anyone's end. The Father so loved the world that He gave His Son to rescue from death all who believe in Him.

## CHAPTER FOUR

# SOME PROBLEMS WITH THE TRADITIONAL VIEW OF HELL

*I*t was only after being convinced of conditionalism's merits from a careful study of key biblical texts that I allowed myself to think about the implications of the ECT theology. Indeed, the realization that cessation of life is the Lord's ultimate solution for the impenitent set me free to consider the traditional view of hell as never before; since it was not God's teaching, I was able to confront the problems of ECT without fear of offending my Savior. Now I wonder how I could have ever attributed ECT to God.

## WAS THE PRODIGAL SON'S FATHER A TRADITIONALIST?

Jesus told the story of a man who had two sons. The younger son requested and received an inheritance from his father and left for a far country where he recklessly squandered everything. Flat broke as a severe famine hit, the prodigal son found himself friendless and starving. In the midst of his suffering, he came to his senses and headed back home. What happens next is one of the most moving pictures in all of scripture:

> And he arose and came to his father. But when he was still a great way off, his father saw him and had compassion, and ran and fell on his neck and kissed him. (Luke 15:20)

Jesus' portrait of the Father is all the more moving in light of a comment made by my Multnomah professor James Braga: "As far as I know, this is the only time in scripture when God was ever said to be in a hurry." God is quick to forgive; He doesn't want to punish. He wants sinners to repent and live. Judgment is only for those who refuse His grace.

Suppose that the prodigal son had refused his father's grace and not returned home. How might the story have ended? Traditionalist theology would have the father telling his older son something like this:

> Your brother is suffering greatly in a far country and near to death due to his waywardness and impenitence. I long for him to return home, but if he doesn't, he deserves far more than a painful death. He deserves to be friendless and in pain forever.

Is it conceivable that the father of the prodigal son would insist that his son suffer without relief for all eternity? Since the penalty for sin must be in keeping with the character of the God who determined it, to find ECT theology to be incompatible with the God revealed in Luke 15 is a significant problem for traditionalism.

## TRADITIONALISM'S INCOMPATIBILITY WITH THE ESSENCE OF CHRISTIANITY

God is not some impersonal force. He is the infinite-personal Creator of the universe. Adam and Eve were created in God's image. This does not mean that they were created all-powerful or all-knowing or immortal. "Man," notes Francis Schaeffer, "being made in the image of God, was made to have a personal relationship with Him,"[1] and not just any personal relationship. God seeks a love relationship. This is why God created humans with free will. "Free will," in the words of C. S. Lewis, "though it makes evil possible, is also the only thing that makes possible any love or goodness or joy worth having."[2] God could have created a world of animated robots and programmed every thought and action to suit His pleasure, but life would then be a meaningless charade. A true love relationship requires two willing partners that freely choose each other.

True love cannot be coerced, yet isn't ECT the ultimate threat? What greater coercion could there possibly be?

Conditional immortality provides strong incentive for accepting Christ, but the death penalty is primarily a matter of justice. A society where crime goes unpunished devolves into chaos and becomes intolerable. God is not like a district attorney that refuses to enforce the law; if there is to be new heavens and a new earth in which righteousness dwells, the penalty for sin must be carried out.

The traditional view of hell fails to keep sin out of God's righteous new universe; furthermore, endless, unbearable pain constitutes utterly unprecedented coercion unbecoming of the genuine love relationship that God desires. If forced love is no love at all, is not ECT incompatible with the essence of Christianity?

## MISLED BY MY KING JAMES BIBLE

The good that has come from the King James Bible is overwhelming, but it's not a perfect translation. We saw this with regard to the mistranslation of Hades in Luke 16. It also let me down in Mark 9.

Reading Mark 9:43 in my King James Bible as a new Christian, I thought I was hearing what Jesus literally said, but that wasn't the case. The description of hell as "the fire that never shall be quenched" is a paraphrase. When Jesus warned against going into hell, he called hell: τὸ πῦρ τὸ ἄσβεστον (SBLGNT)—"the fire— the unquenchable" (YLT).[3]

If the KJV had followed the original text more closely and warned against going "into the unquenchable fire" (NASB), I might have recalled John the Baptist's warning that unquenchable fire will utterly consume the unsaved (Matt. 3:12; Lk. 3:17). Instead, I was set up to arrive at a horrible conclusion.

Conditioned to think that people have to live somewhere forever and reading of a hell where the fire *never* shall end, the words "where their worm dieth not, and the fire is not quenched" (Mk. 9:44, KJV) hit me as a shocking picture of torture. That the KJV repeats the line three times (9:44, 46, 48) when it only occurs once in the original Greek text (something else I didn't realize at the time) only intensified the horror. Throw in my own ignorance of the Old Testament and you have the ingredients for a tragic misunderstanding.

## UNDYING WORM AND UNQUENCHABLE FIRE

When I first read Mark 9, I didn't know that Jesus' warning of hell was illustrated by a gruesome picture of literal physical death from the Book of Isaiah. Biblical prophecy informs us that the armies of the world will invade Israel and attack Jerusalem at the end of the Great Tribulation. These armies will be defeated by Christ in the battle known as Armageddon, leaving a multitude of dead soldiers on Israeli soil. This brings peace to Israel, but it also presents a huge practical problem: How will an unprecedented multitude of dead bodies be cleared from the battlefield? The incredible size of the slaughter (Rev. 14:20) will require a massive cleansing operation. Birds have a role (Rev. 19:11–18), but given the magnitude of the problem, it will surely take more than birds to complete this overwhelming task. Isaiah ends with worshippers, who have come to Jerusalem in the millennial kingdom, going forth to look upon the *corpses* of those slain by the Lord at His return. These *dead bodies* are beset with unquenchable fire and undying worms (Isa. 66:24).

Why *unquenchable* fire and *undying* worms? Picture the historical practice of public cremation where the body is placed on a raised platform with firewood all around to facilitate burning. The effort required to incinerate just *one* body via normal fire calls into question the ability of everyday quenchable fire to consume those slain by the Lord at His return. It will surely take "unquenchable fire" that is impervious to the combustion difficulties presented by massive piles of human corpses. As we saw in chapter one, this is precisely the nature of unquenchable fire in the writings of the Old Testament prophets. *Unquenchable fire is not fire that burns forever; it is fire that cannot be prevented from completing its mission.* Likewise, special worms are logically called for, worms that are as unstoppable as unquenchable fire—*undying* worms.

The aftermath of the Armageddon battlefield will be gruesome, with countless corpses being consumed by vultures, *undying* worms, and *unquenchable* fire. How long this abhorrent scene continues is not stated, but if the land must be cleansed for the blessings of the millennial Messianic kingdom articulated by Isaiah to be realized, does it not follow that fire and worm serve to consume these corpses? Indeed, the prophesied fruitful conditions of the millennium provide confidence that corpses will surely give way to crops (Amos 9:11–15).

### *Unquenchable Fire, Undying Worm, and Mark 9*

When I come to Jesus' teaching on hell in Mark 9:43–48, I look back to Isaiah 66 and see corpses being consumed by fire and worms. Then when I look at biblical statements regarding the unsaved and final judgment fire, I see that Jesus taught that the unsaved would burn up like weeds cast into a furnace of fire. I hear the testimony of John the Baptist that unquenchable fire will burn up the chaff. The traditionalist claim, by contrast, is that the fires of *Gehenna* burn eternally without ever consuming a single sinner, but if we try to apply the traditionalist interpretation of unquenchable fire and undying worm to the millennial kingdom scene of which Isaiah wrote, we have an impossible situation, absurd if you try to envision it.

The traditionalist view is inconsistent with both Isaiah and the explicit statements about God's judgment fire made by Jesus and John the Baptist. Jesus did not choose a portrait of torment to illuminate the danger of *Gehenna*; He chose Isaiah's gruesome picture of literal physical death. Combining Isaiah 66:24 with Mark 9:43–48 and the key passages on hell in Matthew leads to the following conclusion: Just as undying worm and unquenchable fire consume literal corpses in the aftermath of the Battle of Armageddon, sinners cast into the flames of *Gehenna* will be consumed, soul and body.

## LET DOWN BY PASTORS AND TEACHERS

The KJV misinformed us when it said that the rich man was in hell. Most evangelical leaders know the difference between hell and Hades, yet many not only claim that the rich man was in hell but also cite his suffering as a confirmation of their theology. Robert Yarbrough writes,

> Jesus also speaks of hell in Luke's Gospel in the story of the rich man and Lazarus: "In *hell*, where he [the rich man] was in torment, he looked up and saw Abraham far away" ... Significantly, this is yet another passage that

points to a conscious and unending torment endured by hell's inhabitants.[4]

The all-too-common traditionalist assertion that the rich man was in hell is another falsehood that has influenced believers to accept ECT. Declaring temporary suffering in Hades to be eternal suffering in hell accomplishes nothing, except possibly reminding us that traditionalist proof texts do not legitimately affirm their position.

### Thus Says the Lord?

Another common traditionalist practice is to treat paraphrases as the actual words of scripture. A prime example is 2 Thessalonians 1:9, where Paul appears to provide a commentary on Matthew 25:31–46:

> These [who do not obey the Gospel, v8] shall be punished with everlasting destruction from the presence of the Lord and from the glory of His power, when He comes, in that Day, to be glorified in His saints and to be admired among all those who believe, because our testimony among you was believed. (2 Thess. 1:9–10)

How do traditionalists respond to Paul's declaration that unbelievers will be punished with everlasting destruction? Peterson acknowledges that *destruction* could mean annihilation but denies that it carries this sense in 2 Thessalonians 1:9.[5] Peterson offers two reasons in support of his position. His first reason is that "everlasting destruction" would be redundant wording.

> First, the expression "*everlasting* destruction" denotes the never-ending devastation of the unsaved in hell. Contrary to annihilationist claims, "*everlasting* destruction" is a cumbersome way to denote the obliteration of the wicked. If extinction were meant, why not just say "destruction?"[6]

Yet Paul does just say "destruction" in Philippians: "For many walk, of whom I have told you often, and now tell you even weeping, that they are the enemies of the cross of Christ: whose end is *destruction*" (3:18–19). Second, there is precedent for the use of *everlasting* in conjunction with a one-time act of eternal consequence. We observed this previously with regard to eternal redemption. Third, why should it be assumed that "everlasting" is superfluous? Is it unreasonable for Paul to make an emphatic statement in a chapter in which his mind is on the suffering of the church at the hands of unbelievers? Finally, imagine if Paul had written something like "anguishing torment" and a conditionalist argued that Paul really meant "extinction" because "anguishing torment" is cumbersome! Peterson's second reason relies on an NIV paraphrase of Paul's words.

> Second, the latter part of 2 Thessalonians 1:9 supports traditionalism rather than annihilationism. Paul writes, "They will be punished with everlasting destruction and shut out from the presence of the Lord and from the majesty of his power"… Here we learn what "everlasting destruction" entails—the wicked being forever excluded from the gracious presence of the Lord. This cannot be annihilation, for their separation presupposes their existence.[7]

The words "and shut out," which could imply continued existence, are *not* in the Greek text; they reflect the opinion of the NIV translators as to how the verse should be understood. The Greek word *apo* is primarily translated as *from* in the New Testament; *away from* is a common meaning. The NKJV reads, "These shall be punished with everlasting destruction *from* [*apo*] the presence of the Lord and from the glory of His power." The NASB reads, "These people will pay the penalty of eternal destruction, *away from* [*apo*] the presence of the Lord and from the glory of His power." Both translations are best understood in light of Matthew 25.

Sitting on the throne of His glory (Matt. 25:31), the Lord Jesus sends the wicked into the lake of fire (Matt. 25:41) where eternal destruction takes place. Everlasting destruction, then, comes *from* the Lord Jesus. That is, Jesus is responsible for the destruction. It is also true that unbelievers pay the penalty of eternal destruction *away from* the presence of Christ: "Depart *from Me*, you cursed, into the everlasting fire" (Matt. 25:41), into the fire where the chaff "will burn up" (Matt. 3:12).

A literal word-for-word translation of 2 Thessalonians 1:9 does not support the traditionalist view. Peterson says that separation presupposes the ongoing existence of the unsaved, but the separation of which he speaks is based on words not found in the Greek text. Building doctrine on paraphrase is like building a house on sand.

## TRADITIONALIST CONFLICTION IN EVANGELISM

No one has ever given a satisfactory justification for ECT. One evidence of this, I believe, is that traditionalists often feel compelled to close their teaching on hell by saying things like: "God's ways are beyond our understanding," and "We can trust that He will judge righteously." In *Erasing Hell*, Chan writes, "He hasn't asked us to figure out why He does the things He does. We can't. We are not capable. Our thinking is inferior to His."[8] This leads to Chan's suggestion that we "put our energy toward submitting rather than overanalyzing"[9] and "cling to Abraham's words in Genesis 18:25: 'Shall not the Judge of all the earth do what is just?'"[10]

But is this a responsible approach to doctrine and theology? Is final judgment not to be understood in this life? Henry Constable writes,

> We are often told that, while no doubt God's conduct towards sinners will one day appear to the redeemed and even to the lost to have been just, yet that we must be content *to wait* until it shall so appear. This life is to pass away, the hour of resurrection must come, the throne of judgment must be set, the guilt of the lost be displayed, the everlasting sentence be passed, *and then*, the redeemed and the lost alike will see that God's ways were just. Not so, we reply. God appeals to us *now* to judge.... When the judgment is set, and the sentence passed, *it is too late*.[11]

Jesus came to reveal the Father to a broken world. He went to where people lived, broke bread with them, heard their concerns, answered their questions, healed the sick, gave sight to the blind, demonstrated the magnificence of God's grace at Calvary, and brought hope of immortality by rising from the dead. Josh McDowell would call it evidence that demands a verdict. Is the same not true of the penalty for sin from which Jesus rescues believers? Is not divine justice a revelation of God's character that also demands a verdict? Constable continues,

> But they who tell us to *wait in faith* wholly miscalculate the real position of the question before us…. God's character and conduct are to win faith; not to be sustained by faith against appearances. The missionary tells the unbeliever what kind of God the God of the Christian is, to convert the unbeliever to the faith.[12]

In the comfort of their own fellowships, traditionalists may be able to dodge the injustice of their position through blind faith, but this strategy doesn't work when it comes to evangelism. It is the *goodness* of God that leads to repentance (Rom. 2:4). God "did not leave Himself without witness, in that He *did good*" (Acts 14:17). "We love Him because He first *loved* us" (1 Jn. 4:19). These truths are so powerful that most traditionalists abandon ECT when asking the unsaved to believe in Christ.

*Erasing Hell* ends with an invitation to respond to God in love and trust. Interestingly, Chan's *"Finally … Are You Sure?"* conclusion (perhaps unconsciously) adopts conditionalist language when calling people to trust Christ: "And so we all have a choice before us. Choose life or choose death."[13] Traditionalists understand the second death to represent ECT. Moreover, Chan strongly urges that it is time to stop being embarrassed and stop trying to "cover" for God,[14] so why doesn't Chan state that the choice is between eternal life and eternal suffering? It could be because it is awkward to speak metaphorically of death as endless misery while sharing the story of Christ's literal crucifixion, literal burial, literal empty tomb, and literal bodily resurrection. Primarily, though, to verbalize God's love for people and the eternal torment of sons and daughters and mothers and fathers *in the same breath* is simply too incoherent.

Conditionalists need not hesitate to affirm their understanding of final judgment when sharing the Gospel. The essence of conditionalism is evident in verses such as Romans 6:23 and John 3:16. Traditionalists typically remain conflicted, holding to ECT in doctrinal statements while avoiding its mention when doing evangelism.

## ABOUT CHURCH TRADITION

It is common to hear traditionalists say that ECT has been *the* teaching of the Church for the past 2000 years. How true is this?

During the early centuries of church history, there was no consensus on the doctrine of hell. There were three major views: conditionalism, universalism, and ECT. Advocates of conditionalism include Ignatius, Irenaeus, and Arnobius; universalism was preached by influential church fathers such as Origen and Gregory of Nyssa; Athenagoras, Tertullian, and Augustine held to ECT.

It was not until the church at Rome came to rule over other churches that ECT became the dominant view. Augustine's view was the one adopted by the Roman Catholic Church, which affirmed and propagated ECT for the next thousand years of church history. The traditional view of hell also prevailed during the Reformation although conditionalism was favored by many of "the radical reformers known as Anabaptists."[15] Dubbed "rebaptizers" by those who practiced infant baptism, Anabaptists held that baptism was for adults who believed in Christ and were determined to follow Him. In stark contrast to the Roman Catholic Church, Anabaptists rejected the union of church and state. As Abraham, Isaac, and Jacob dwelt in tents waiting for God's heavenly city, Anabaptists saw themselves as pilgrims and the church as "an association of perpetual aliens."[16] Opposed by Luther, Calvin, and Catholics, Anabaptists experienced brutal persecution. John Yoder and Alan Kreider write,

> By 1527 they [the Reformers] had determined to use all necessary means to root out Anabaptism. They were joined in this determination by the Catholic authorities. To Protestants and Catholics alike, the Anabaptists seemed not only to be dangerous heretics; they also seemed to threaten the religious and social stability of Christian Europe. In the carnage of the next quarter of a century thousands of Anabaptists were put to death (by fire in the Catholic territories, by drowning and the sword under Protestant regimes). Thousands more saved their skins by recanting.[17]

Rather than learning from each other, sadly, blood was shed and a unique opportunity for theological discourse was missed. The modern era has seen a slow but steady advancement of conditionalism.

In the nineteenth century, conditionalism was embraced by the Advent Christian Church, a member of the National Association of Evangelicals, as well as numerous scholars including Henry Constable and R. F. Weymouth. During the twentieth century, opposition to ECT was especially strong in England. Harold Guillebaud, Basil Atkinson, John Wenham, and John Stott are among those who made the case for conditionalism. A sense of the exegetically robust international rejection of ECT is captured in *Rethinking Hell: Readings in Evangelical Conditionalism*. In this excellent collection of writings, conditionalism is affirmed by the aforementioned British scholars and a host of others, including E. Earle Ellis, Philip Hughes, and Edward Fudge. John Stackhouse Jr. writes,

> There are chapters upon chapters of high-quality argument: exegesis of Scriptures, logical deductions, inferences to best explanations, metaphors and thought experiments, and more. I've never seen such a book, in fact, that piled up such a rich array of reasons to hold to a particular theological idea.[18]

In 2000, the Evangelical Alliance Commission on Unity and Truth among Evangelicals (ACUTE), under the auspices of the Evangelical Alliance, the largest and oldest association of evangelicals in the U. K., released a report entitled *The Nature of Hell*. The report states,

> The interpretation of hell in terms of conditional immortality is a significant minority evangelical view. Furthermore, we believe that the traditionalist-conditionalist debate on hell should be regarded as a secondary rather than a primary

issue for evangelical theology. Although hell is a profoundly serious matter, we view the holding of either one of these two views of it over against the other to be neither essential in respect of Christian doctrine, nor finally definitive of what it means to be an evangelical Christian.[19]

Just a few years ago, in America, the popular, theologically conservative, evangelical ministry GotQuestions.org echoed the ACUTE position. The ministry holds to the traditional view of hell but affirms conditional immortality to be a valid alternative for Christians. Believing that it is good for one's viewpoint to be challenged, the ministry posted an article that positively presents the conditionalist position.[20] This stance by GotQuestions.org is a breath of fresh air in a country that has historically struggled to attain to the biblical precedent set by the Bereans when it comes to the doctrine of hell.

As awareness of conditionalism's history and legitimacy grows, we should hear fewer and fewer traditionalists claiming that ECT has been *the* teaching of the church for 2000 years. Appreciation of conditional immortality's incredible harmony with Christ's sacrifice at Calvary is also long overdue.

## THE PRICE OF REDEMPTION

Have you ever noticed that evangelicals say that sinners deserve to *suffer forever* but Christ paid our penalty by *dying* for us? Living forever in pain and dying are two entirely different things, yet traditionalists appear oblivious to the contradiction. If eternal suffering is the penalty for sin as traditionalists claim, then nobody's sins are paid for because the suffering of Jesus at the cross was neither infinite nor eternal.

Some traditionalists are under the impression that Christ as God "could endure infinite and eternal punishment in a finite time and specific place."[21] But scripture is explicit that Christ paid for our sins in His humanity: "who Himself bore our sins *in His own body* on the tree" (1 Pet. 2:24). Indeed, the eternal Son "became flesh and dwelt among us" (Jn. 1:14) to accomplish what was otherwise impossible for Him to do: die for sinners. Jesus "was made a little lower than the angels, *for the suffering of death…that He…might taste death for everyone*" (Heb. 2:9). Further, the notion that Christ, in His divine nature, suffered separation from the Father fails to take into consideration that the divine essence is not divisible but one (Deut. 6:4; Jam. 2:19). The idea that the Trinity was torn apart at the cross is preposterous, yet this is where ECT theology has taken some traditionalists.

The closest traditionalists can come to harmonizing their understanding of the penalty for sin with the crucifixion of Christ is to argue, as Peterson does in *Two Views of Hell*, that "because of the infinite dignity of Christ's person, his sufferings, though finite in duration, were of infinite weight on the scales of divine justice."[22] This does not represent fully the reality of Calvary, however. At the cross, Jesus experienced intense suffering followed by literal bodily death verified by burial in Joseph of Arimathea's tomb. Conditionalism adheres to this pattern by affirming the suffering of the unsaved, appropriate to one's sin, followed by death. ECT theology is a matter of suffering followed only by more suffering.

A review of God's plan of redemption will reveal yet another profound parallel between the death of Christ and conditionalism.

## The Payment Made: The Precious Blood of Christ

God's salvation is by blood: "When I see the *blood*, I will pass over you," says the Lord (Ex. 12:13). Paul writes, "In Him we have *redemption through His blood*, the forgiveness of sins, according to the riches of His grace" (Eph. 1:7). Peter writes, "You were not redeemed with perishable things like silver or gold from your futile way of life inherited from your forefathers, but with *precious blood*, as of a lamb unblemished and spotless, *the blood of Christ*" (1 Pet. 1:18–19, NASB). Scripture unequivocally proclaims, "it is the blood that makes atonement for the soul" (Lev. 17:11). No other price can secure forgiveness.

Ponder it: The Judge of all the earth neither requires nor is satisfied by eternal suffering: "apart from blood-shedding forgiveness doth not come" (Heb. 9:22, YLT).

## A Sacrifice to be Accepted

It may have appeared, while His disfigured, lifeless body hung on the cross, as if Christ had been defeated by the world; in truth, when Jesus laid down His holy, undefiled life for Adam's fallen race, He accomplished a great redemptive victory. Having completed the mission given to Him by the Father, Jesus was free to enter Paradise (Lk. 23:43). On the third day, Jesus' tomb was found empty. "He is not here," said the angels, "but is risen!" (Lk. 24:1–7). The peace made by the blood of Jesus' cross countered the world's transgressions (Col. 1:20; 2 Cor. 5:19) and made the acceptance or rejection of the risen Christ the crucial issue in salvation.

To believe in Christ brings life (Jn. 1:12, 20:30–31). To reject Christ is to face final judgment without the benefit of Jesus' shed blood. Christ paid the price of redemption, but His sacrifice needs to be embraced by faith. This is illustrated in Exodus 12 where the blood of the sacrificed lamb had to be put on the lintel and two doorposts of one's house. It is also seen in Jesus' bread of life teaching: "I am the living bread which came down from heaven. *If* anyone *eats* of this bread, he will live forever; and the bread that I shall give is My flesh, which I shall give for the life of the world" (Jn. 6:51). The unbeliever, then, ultimately dies a *redemptionless* death in the lake of fire.

## *A Life Laid Down, Ended*

In Leviticus 16, to make atonement for the people of Israel, Aaron was instructed to kill the goat chosen to be a sin offering and bring its blood into the Holy of Holies to sprinkle it on and before the mercy seat. The blood was a witness that the goat had died; its life was over, come to an end. Since blood sustains the life of the flesh (Lev. 17:14), it could not be otherwise. William R. Newell writes,

> The conception that Christ on the cross was enduring all
> the agonies of the elect for all eternity grew directly out

of the Romish legalism from which the Reformers did not escape ... The shed blood brought in before God on the Day of Atonement simply witnessed that a life had been laid down, ended.[23]

Note the consistency of God's Word. Cessation or end of life is the biblical definition of death, and it is the penalty God requires for sin. It is also the price Christ paid for our sins. The eternal Son left the glories of heaven for a manger in Bethlehem. He became incarnate to obtain a life that could be laid down, ended, for you and me through death at Calvary. When Jesus voluntarily gave up His spirit and breathed His last, His earthly flesh-and-blood life literally came to an end.

Once, Jesus grew and developed like the children in your neighborhood and mine; once, Jesus got weary walking the roads of Israel and experienced hunger and thirst like any man. These things are now but a part of history. Newell says of Christ's resurrection,

> It was not back into the old flesh and blood earthly existence that He came. He had, indeed, His body: "Handle Me and see." "Have ye here anything to eat?" Yet He had poured out His blood. The life of the flesh was in the blood (Lev. 17:11). He had laid that life down. He is now a heavenly Man. He is in the heavenlies.[24]

Jesus went to the cross in His earthly flesh-and-blood life; He rose in His glorious (Phil. 3:21), heavenly (1 Cor. 15:45–49), flesh-and-bone (Lk. 24:39) life. Arthur Jackson writes,

When Christ arose after His death and burial, He ushered in a whole new sphere of reality, a new creation that had not existed before....

His was now a "glorious body;" a body consisting of flesh and bones but—with no blood.... God said of the natural man that the life was in the blood (Gen. 9:4). In the resurrected Christ we see something the world had never encountered before. Here is life on an entirely different principle: a body, a true physical body, immortal, incorruptible, one suited for both heaven and eternity.[25]

The reality that a life ended at the cross is consistent with the conditionalist view that the penalty for sin requires a life to cease. The wonder of God's grace is this: *Jesus died a redemptive death at Calvary that we might not die a redemptionless death in the lake of fire.*

Jesus' shed blood is redemptive both because of who He is and because His blood speaks of a life sacrificially ended for sinners. As the blood of the sacrificed goat testified that its life had ended, so the pouring out of Jesus' blood signified that His earthly life had ended. That He might bring us to God, the body of the righteous One was put to death for the unrighteous (Col. 1:22; 1 Pet. 3:18). Jesus died for us because He doesn't want my life or your life to end in the flames of *Gehenna*. He loves us. He doesn't want us to perish. He wants us to believe in Him and live.

Conditional immortality is not only plainly taught in scripture, its understanding of the fate of the unsaved is fundamentally consistent with Calvary in two ways. As Jesus experienced intense suffering followed by literal bodily death, conditionalism likewise affirms suffering, appropriate to one's sin, followed by death. Conditionalism also shares a parallel with Calvary in that as Christ's earthly flesh-and-blood life ended forever at the cross, so in the second death the impenitent come to a permanent end.

## TRULY FULL OF PROBLEMS

Traditionalism is bursting with problems. I'm glad I don't have to defend the view anymore. Traditionalists think that conditionalists have a couple of problems of their own when it comes to the book of Revelation. In the next chapter, we'll see whether or not that's the case.

## CHAPTER FIVE

# THE REVELATION PASSAGES

*I*n *Hell under Fire*, Gregory Beale calls Revelation 14:11 and 20:10–15 "the Achilles' heel of the annihilationist perspective."[1] Beale obviously feels that conditionalists lack a good answer for these scriptures. Does he have a point?

If we exclude the era of the church fathers, most advocates of conditional immortality, thus far, have been amillennialists (those that do not believe in a literal thousand-year reign of Christ on earth). They have done a tremendous job of making the case for conditionalism, but if the book of Revelation is intended to be understood from a premillennial futurist perspective, it is understandable that the Revelation passages might have been a weakness in most conditionalist literature. When it comes to Revelation 14:11, amillennial conditionalists can point to Isaiah 34:8–10 where brimstone, burning pitch, and smoke that ascends "forever" combine to picture utter devastation. Portraying the torment of the devil, beast, and false prophet in Revelation 20:10 as a figurative symbol representing annihilation, however, admittedly appears to avoid rather than explain the passage.

Conditionalists might not have addressed the Revelation passages satisfactorily, but this should not have prevented their position from being accepted. As Edward Fudge asks,

> Is one supposed to conclude that dozens, even scores and more of simple, declaratory statements throughout all of Scripture must finally be ignored because of fewer than five symbolic verses in Revelation? It makes far better sense to read these few apocalyptic statements written in symbolic language in light of the clear, repeated, consistent teaching from throughout all the rest of Scripture.[2]

Fudge is certainly correct that the overall teaching of scripture should inform one's interpretive conclusions, but when Revelation 14 and 20 are considered from a futuristic perspective, we will yet again find that traditionalist proof texts do not actually say what traditionalists claim they do.

As seen in the following outline, the futurist view holds that most of the events in the book of Revelation take place in the future.

## OUTLINE OF REVELATION

Jesus Himself gave us the broad outline of Revelation when He said to John, "Write the things which you *have seen*, and the things *which are*, and the things which *will take place after this*" (Rev. 1:19).

John had an encounter with Christ in 1:9–20 that fulfills "the things which you have seen." The seven letters to seven churches in chapters 2 and 3 constitute "the things which are." A prologue in chapters 4 and 5 opens the futuristic portion of the book, "the things which will take place." Chapters 6 through 18 detail the Tribulation that precedes the return of Christ in chapter 19. The restraint and torment of Satan, the millennium, and the Great White Throne judgment are found in chapter 20. The new earth and New Jerusalem are the primary focus of chapter 21 and 22:1–5, followed by an epilogue.[3]

## JESUS' MATTHEW 24 GUIDE TO REVELATION

In Matthew 24:3, the disciples ask Jesus: "What will be the sign of Your coming, and of the end of the age?" Jesus answered by warning His disciples of false Christs, wars, famines, pestilences, and earthquakes (vv. 5–7), which He called "the beginning of the birth pains" (v. 8, ESV). Jesus went on to cite the "abomination of desolation" standing in the holy place, foretold by Daniel, as the event that would trigger a period of unprecedented tribulation (vv. 15–21). Christ's return immediately follows the conclusion of this great tribulation (vv. 29–30). Thus, there are two distinct periods of tribulation with the abomination of desolation event spoken of by Daniel in between. It is commonly understood that both periods of tribulation last for forty-two months (3½ years). Futurists typically use the term Tribulation when referring to the entire seven years of tribulation and the term Great Tribulation when referring just to the unprecedented tribulation that immediately precedes Christ's return.

## THE IMPORTANCE OF REVELATION, A PERSONAL WORD

The final years before Christ's return to the earth is a fascinating study for us today, but the truth of Revelation will be invaluable for those living during the Tribulation. This really hit me back in the 1980's. I was witnessing to a friend but without success. At the end of our conversation, I told him about the Rapture of the church and said that if one day Christians were missing all over the world and he couldn't find me, he'd know that what I had been telling him about God and Jesus was true. It was then that I first had a desire to write a book.

At the time of the Rapture, believers will be caught up into the sky to meet Christ in the air and forever be with Him (1 Thess. 4:7). Sometime thereafter the Tribulation will begin (1 Thess. 5:1–9), so if my friend's unbelief continued, it was entirely possible that he could end up in the Tribulation. Should that happen, I wanted him to understand the situation he was in. This chapter in *Eternal by Choice* goes a long way toward accomplishing that goal.

## REVELATION 14:9–11

Then a third angel followed them, saying with a loud voice, "If anyone *worships the beast and his image,* and *receives his mark on his forehead* or *on his hand,* he himself shall also drink of the wine of the wrath of God, which is poured out full strength into the cup of His indignation. He shall be tormented with fire and brimstone in the presence of the holy angels and in the presence of the Lamb. And the *smoke* of their torment ascends forever and ever; and they have no rest day or night, *who worship the beast and his image, and whoever receives the mark of his name.*"

God's wrath in Revelation 14:9–11 is explicitly toward those who worship the beast and receive his mark on the forehead or hand. By beginning and ending with this fact, the passage emphasizes that the wrath in question applies to a specific group of sinners. We are also dealing with a restricted time frame. Worshipping the beast and receiving his mark on the forehead or hand is a possibility only during the forty-two months of the Great Tribulation (Rev. 13:5, 11–18). The uniqueness of this moment is reinforced by the immediate context to which we now turn.

## THE FIVE ANGELS OF REVELATION 14 – THE IMMEDIATE CONTEXT

The warning against worshipping the beast is found in the midst of a series of angelic utterances. Five angels speak in Revelation 14, one after another. John first sees a *flying angel* preaching a message for the entire world: "Fear God and give glory to Him, for the hour of His judgment has come; and worship Him who made heaven and earth, the sea and springs of water" (14:7). To what judgment does the flying angel refer? Peterson believes the final judgment is in view:

The angel who flies in midair announces, "Fear God and give him glory, because the hour of his judgment has come" (Rev 14:7). This refers to the Last Judgment, because the punishment of the wicked described three verses later lasts forever: "The smoke of their torment rises for ever and ever. There is no rest day or night" (v. 11).[4]

There is a key discrepancy, however, between the final judgment in the Bible and the message of the first angel. In Revelation 20:11–15, those who stand before God's Great White Throne are judged to demonstrate that they deserve to be cast into the lake of fire. In stark contrast, the angel in Revelation 14:6–7 presents an opportunity for salvation. The angel flies in midair with "the everlasting gospel to preach to those who dwell on the earth—to every nation, tribe, tongue, and people" (14:6), calling people to "worship Him who made heaven and earth, the sea and springs of water" (14:7). Charles Ryrie states, "The message of this gospel is to all the world. It is God's last call of grace to a world that persists in rejecting Him and that openly defies Him."[5] H. A. Ironside writes,

> It is mercy indeed, to God's creatures everywhere, that in that hour of judgment, before the last blow falls, the call will still go forth to men everywhere to own the claims of the Omnipotent One whose mercies have been rejected so long.[6]

There is no flying angel preaching from the skies today, nor does the angel's message fit the conditions of the Messianic millennium or the new earth. Futurists have long maintained that the angelic preaching of Revelation 14:6–7 is an event exclusive to the Tribulation preceding Christ's return.

A *second angel* announces the fall of Babylon (14:8). This proclamation is also fulfilled during the Tribulation (Rev. 16:19).

The *third angel* warns against worshipping the beast and receiving his mark on the forehead or hand. Those who follow the beast will reap the wrath of God. *When, where, and how long this wrath occurs is the focus of our present investigation.*

A *fourth angel* cries in a loud voice to One like the Son of Man (seated on a white cloud), "Thrust in Your sickle and reap, for the time has come for You to reap, for the harvest of the earth is ripe" (14:15). In response, "He who sat on the cloud thrust in His sickle on the earth, and the earth was reaped" (14:16). A *fifth angel* cries out to an angel with a sharp sickle (introduced in 14:17) to "thrust in your sharp sickle and gather the clusters of the vine of the earth, for her grapes are fully ripe" (Rev. 14:18). The angel throws the harvested vine of the earth into the great winepress of the wrath of God, and blood flows for a distance of about 184 miles (14:19–20). The fourth and fifth angels also speak of judgment that finds its fulfillment on earth, this time at the return of Christ (Rev. 19:11–21).

In Revelation 14, we find a series of angels speaking about judgment. The first, second, fourth, and fifth angels tell of judgment that begins and ends on earth. Because consistency would suggest that the third angel's judgment is temporal, let's outline the passage and investigate whether or not there is a correlation between Revelation 14:9–11 and the events of the Great Tribulation.

## OUTLINE OF THE PASSAGE

I see the passage break down in the following way:

- VERSE 9 *sets the stage:* Then a third angel followed them, saying with a loud voice, "If anyone worships the beast and his image, and receives his mark on his forehead or on his hand,"

- VERSE 10A *is a broad picture of wrath:* "he himself shall also drink of the wine of the wrath of God, which is poured out full strength into the cup of His indignation."

- VERSES 10B and 11A *spotlight a specific aspect of wrath:* "He shall be tormented with fire and brimstone in the presence of the holy angels and in the presence of the Lamb. And the smoke of their torment ascends forever and ever;"

- VERSE 11B *is a broad summary statement:* "and they have no rest day or night, who worship the beast and his image, and whoever receives the mark of his name."

## REVELATION 14:9–11 AND THE EVENTS OF THE GREAT TRIBULATION

First, there is a thematic match between the third angel's message and the Great Tribulation trumpet and bowl judgments. The third angel warns of the wrath of God, which is the implicit theme of the trumpet judgments and the explicit theme of the bowl judgments.

> Then I saw another sign in heaven, great and marvelous: *seven angels* having the *seven last plagues,* for *in them* the *wrath of God* is complete. (Rev. 15:1)

> Then I heard a loud voice from the temple saying to the
> *seven angels*, "Go and *pour out the bowls* of the *wrath of
> God* on the earth." (Rev. 16:1)

Second, fire and brimstone are key aspects of the third
angel's message and God's Great Tribulation fury. The Great
Tribulation begins and ends with judgment by fire. Fire plays
a prominent role in the *first trumpet judgment*, burning up a
third of the trees and all green grass (8:7). The *second trumpet* involves "something like a great mountain burning with
fire" (8:8). The *third trumpet* sounds, and "a great star fell
from heaven, burning like a torch" (8:10). The *fourth trumpet*
results in a one-third reduction of light from the sun, moon,
and stars (8:12). The *fifth trumpet* brings five months of torment via demonic locust beings to those "who do not have
the seal of God" (9:1–12). Fire, smoke, and brimstone are
explicitly named in the *sixth trumpet* judgment (9:17). This
wrath is so intense that a third of humankind will die (9:18).

In the *bowl judgments*, "a foul and loathsome sore"
comes "upon the men who had the mark of the beast and
those who worshiped his image" (16:2), waters are turned to
blood to punish those who "have shed the blood of saints and
prophets" (16:4–6), fierce heat scorches the impenitent (16:9),
and painful darkness, reminiscent of the ninth Mosaic plague,
afflicts the beast's kingdom (16:10; cf. Ex. 10:21). The final
bowl is undoubtedly poured out just prior to Christ's return
and includes the fact that "great Babylon was remembered
before God, to give her the cup of the wine of the fierceness
of His wrath" (16:19). The inclusion of the fall of Babylon in

the final bowl is significant because the judgment of Babylon explicitly involves not only torment and destruction by fire (18:8–10, 15–21) but also smoke that rises "forever and ever" (19:3).

Third, it makes sense that smoke would literally rise continually while judgments involving fire and sulfur bring pain and suffering to beast worshippers during the Great Tribulation.

Fourth, the third angel states that torment by fire and brimstone takes place "in the presence of the holy angels." The connection between the torment of the rebellious during the Great Tribulation and the holy angels is clear and undeniable. The trumpets are sounded by holy angels, and the bowls are poured out by holy angels.

Fifth, torment by fire and brimstone also takes place "in the presence of the Lamb." This makes good sense in the context of the Great Tribulation; after all, the holy angels who sound the trumpets and pour out the bowls of wrath serve the Lamb.

Sixth, God's wrath is relentless in the third angel's message: "And they have no rest day or night, who worship the beast and his image, and whoever receives the mark of his name" (Rev. 14:11b). Similarly, the trumpet and bowl judgments ensure wave after wave of tribulation for beast worshippers. The relentlessness of God's wrath in the Great Tribulation is perhaps best captured by the Bible's birth-pangs metaphor. There is an obvious parallel between the two stages of a pregnant woman's labor (early and active) and the two stages of tribulation that precede Christ's return to the earth (beginning birth pangs and unprecedented tribulation). As a woman's contractions become increasingly regular and stronger during the active labor stage of her pregnancy, so those who worship the beast and take his mark will have no relief from God's wrath during the Great Tribulation.

There is a clear connection between the third angel's message and the Great Tribulation; unfortunately, it is rarely acknowledged. Though futuristic traditionalists recognize the Great Tribulation setting of Revelation 14, verses 9–11 are typically assumed to be talking about the lake of fire. A key supporting factor for both amillennial and premillennial traditionalists is the Greek phrase typically translated "forever and ever."

## DOES "FOREVER AND EVER" NECESSARILY DENOTE ETERNITY?

Peterson writes, "The expression 'for ever and ever' occurs thirteen times in Revelation and each time denotes eternity."[7] Usually, "forever and ever" does involve eternity in the book of Revelation. This is because the phrase is primarily linked to the eternal Creator. In Revelation 5:13, for example, we read, "To him who sits on the throne and to the Lamb be praise and honor and glory and power, for ever and ever!" (NIV). But must "forever and ever" always encompass eternity?

Vine states that the various "forever and ever" phrases formed in connection with *aion*, an age, "are idiomatic expressions betokening undefined periods."[8] While studying Matthew 10:28, I had discovered that W. E. Vine was a staunch traditionalist, so Vine's acknowledgment that *forever and ever* doesn't necessarily mean eternal really grabbed my attention. Similarly, traditionalist Gregory Beale acknowledges in *Hell under Fire* that *forever and ever* is a "temporal phrase" and affirms that whether or not eternity is in view depends on the "context of the passage and of the book."[9] Taken together, these traditionalist scholars inform us that *forever and ever* is an undefined period, the duration of which is contextually determined. If this is correct, then the many examples of *forever and ever* linked to the eternal God do not determine the meaning of *forever and ever* in Revelation 14:11. Every instance of the phrase must be considered in its own context.

The common characteristic of the *forever and ever* passages seems to be that something is constant. Praise and honor and glory and power continually, *always*, belong to God. Regarding the smoke that "ascends" forever and ever in Revelation 14:11, Greek scholar Fritz Rienecker notes that the present tense of ascend connected with "the temporal designation 'forever' indicates a continual unbroken action."[10] The devil, the beast, and the false prophet will experience torment *day and night*.

In considering the possibility that *forever and ever* in Revelation 14:11 indicates that smoke will ascend continually from fire and brimstone judgments that torment beast worshippers during the Great Tribulation, any other examples of *forever and ever* linked to rising smoke would be of the utmost importance. We have such an instance in Revelation 19:3. Does the smoke rising "forever and ever" from fallen Babylon rise eternally?

# HER SMOKE RISES FOREVER AND EVER

The fall of Babylon occurs at the end of the Great Tribulation (Rev. 16:17–19). Revelation 17:1–19:3 describes in detail the judgment of Babylon, the great harlot, declaring her final and complete destruction, which includes smoke that rises up "forever and ever." Here is part of the revelation given to John:

> And *she will be utterly burned with fire*, for strong is the Lord God who judges her. The kings of the earth who committed fornication and lived luxuriously with her will weep and lament for her, when they see *the smoke of her burning*, standing at a distance for fear of her torment, saying, "Alas, alas, that *great city Babylon*, that *mighty city*! For in one hour your judgment has come." (18:8–10)

> Every shipmaster, all who travel by ship, sailors, and as many as trade on the sea, stood at a distance and cried out when they saw *the smoke of her burning* (18:17b-18a)

> Then a mighty angel took up a stone like a great millstone and threw it into the sea, saying, "Thus with violence *the great city* Babylon shall be thrown down, and *shall not be found anymore*." (18:21)

This revelation is in keeping with Isaiah's prophecy that Babylon would be "as when God overthrew Sodom and Gomorrah" (Isa. 13:19). As Abraham looked toward the cities of Sodom and Gomorrah and saw "the smoke of the land which went up like the smoke of a furnace" (Gen. 19:28), eyewitnesses substantiate the literalness of Babylon's burning.

The smoke rising from the city of Babylon at the end of the Great Tribulation, which confirmed the termination of the great harlot who shed the blood of prophets and saints, is cause for rejoicing in heaven:

> After these things I heard a loud voice of a great multitude in heaven, saying, "Alleluia! Salvation and glory and honor and power belong to the Lord our God! For true and righteous are His judgments, because He has judged the great harlot who corrupted the earth with her fornication; and He has avenged on her the blood of His servants shed by her." Again they said, "Alleluia! Her *smoke rises up forever and ever*!" (Rev. 19:1–3)

The smoke that causes the kings, shipmasters, and sailors to mourn in Revelation 18 is said, in Revelation 19:3, to rise forever and ever, yet the smoke resulting from the destruction of the city of Babylon during the Tribulation will surely not rise endlessly. Surely it will not cloud the renewed earth during the Messianic millennial reign of Christ (Rev. 20:4–6) or pollute the new earth (Rev. 21:1). Thus, it appears that Vine and Beale are correct that "forever and ever" does not necessarily denote eternity but requires contextual verification as to the time frame involved.

This really shouldn't surprise us; "forever" in the Old Testament does not necessarily mean eternal, either. The law concerning bond servants stipulated that one could voluntarily become a servant *forever* to a fellow Israelite (Deut. 15:12–17), yet this relationship lasted only for a temporal earthly lifetime. Israel was promised land with specific boundaries "forever" (Gen. 13:14–15, 15:18), but this will end when the present earth passes away. In the new earth, all things are made new (Rev. 21:1–5).

The smoke of Revelation 19:3 may not rise eternally, but we can expect it to rise continually while Babylon burns. With this scriptural understanding of "forever and ever" when paired with rising smoke fresh in our minds, let us review the setting and message of Revelation 14:9–11.

## THE MESSAGE OF REVELATION 14:9–11

In Revelation 13, pressure from Satan to worship the beast intensely endangers life and livelihood. Those that refuse to worship the image of the beast will be killed (vv. 11–15), and those that refuse to take the mark of the beast will be denied the right to engage in commerce (vv. 16–17). In Revelation 14, the everlasting gospel is preached to the world: "Fear God and give glory to Him, for the hour of His judgment has come; and worship Him who made heaven and earth, the sea and springs of water" (v. 7). Thus, leading up to Revelation 14:9–11, two distinct paths emerge: Worship the beast or worship Him who made heaven and earth.

Should we be surprised if the third angel of Revelation 14 should warn of relentless wrath and suffering in the immediate present for those that choose to worship the beast and take his mark? This is certainly what happens in the chapters surrounding Revelation 14. Unleashing devastation and torment and death on the earth—one trumpet sounds after another. One by one, the bowls of the wrath of God are poured out. In the Great Tribulation, "they have no respite day and night who do homage to the beast and to its image" (Rev. 14:11b, Darby Translation).

Traditionalists claim that the lake of fire is in view in Revelation 14:9–11, but their only rationale for this is the notion that "forever and ever" must mean eternal, which simply isn't true. If smoke can rise "forever and ever" (i.e., continually) from burning Babylon prior to the return of Christ, then it can surely rise "forever and ever" (continually) from fire and brimstone judgments that torment beast worshippers during the Great Tribulation.

The choice set before the world during the Great Tribulation is intense and urgent: Worship the beast or worship "Him who made heaven and earth, the sea and springs of water" (Rev. 14:7). According to ECT theology, God counters Satan's intense tangible pressure with the threat of suffering in the next world, but this doesn't fit the unique circumstances of the Great Tribulation. Revelation 14:9–11 promises not ECT beyond the grave but relentless wrath and suffering *on earth* for those who reject God.

## REVELATION 20:10

> The *devil*, who deceived them, was cast into the lake of fire
> and brimstone where the beast and the false prophet are.
> And they will be tormented day and night forever and ever.

Evil must be judged, and there is no greater evil in the universe than Satan. Inasmuch as Satan, the beast (also known as Antichrist), and the false prophet forcibly lead the world away from God, it is especially appropriate that this unholy trio suffer without respite in the lake of fire while unsaved men and women appear before God's Great White Throne for final judgment. Is there more to Revelation 20:10 than this? Does this verse about the devil and his cohorts teach that human beings who reject Christ will experience unrelenting torment throughout eternity?

If we are to understand John's vision, we need an accurate assessment of the devil, the beast, and the false prophet. Few question the identity of the devil, but the beast like a leopard with feet like a bear and a mouth like that of a lion, this creature with seven heads and ten horns (Rev. 13:1–7) that John saw in the lake of fire—who is this?

## THE BEAST IS INTRODUCED BY DANIEL

It is commonly understood by futurists that the beast is a man, referred to in Daniel 9 as the "prince who is to come" (v. 26), that heads a group of nations that essentially represents a second coming of the Roman Empire. As the leader of this empire, Antichrist enters into a seven-year covenant or treaty with the nation of Israel. The signing of this covenant marks the beginning of the Tribulation.

### The Two Stages of the Beast's Rule

During the first half of the Tribulation, Antichrist is the leader of a ten-nation confederation (Rev. 17:12–13), but he is a global authority during the Great Tribulation. The beast's transition from a regional power to ruling the world is the work of Satan: "The dragon gave him his power, his throne, and great authority" (Rev. 13:2); "authority was given him over every tribe, tongue, and nation" (Rev. 13:7). Antichrist's world rule continues until he is defeated by Christ and cast into the lake of fire (Rev. 19:19–20). Since it is clearly a man that signs the treaty with Israel that starts the Tribulation, futuristic traditionalists see Satan and two human beings suffering for a thousand years in the lake of fire in Revelation 20:10.

If we had only Daniel to guide us, seeing two human beings suffering in the lake of fire along with Satan would be understandable. New information about Antichrist provided exclusively by the book of Revelation, however, leads to a different conclusion. This new information is critical to discovering the true identity of the strange-looking beast that John saw in the lake of fire.

## JOHN'S VISON OF THE BEAST

John brings us brand new information about Antichrist: At the midpoint of the Tribulation, the beast will die and come back to life (Rev. 13:3–5, 12–14). A few have suggested that this might refer to the beast's kingdom rather than to the beast himself. But the idea that Antichrist's regional empire, which will exercise significant power at the start of the Tribulation, is to be destroyed and suddenly reestablished to rule the world is unrealistic. Futurists overwhelmingly agree that the mortal wound applies to Antichrist himself. Newell states, "One who has been slain with the death-stroke of a sword is 'healed'; a killed body stands up!"[11] Some surmise that the death is faked, but the evidence is strong that the beast actually dies. Joseph Seiss says of the lethal wound,

It is further described as a sword-wound, "the stroke of his death," or a stroke which carries death to him who experiences it.... Similar phraseology is used in this Book with regard to Christ [Rev. 5:6], but all agree that it there means return to life by resurrection after a real bodily killing. How, then, can it mean less here?[12]

Since Antichrist is a man whose prophesied career continues through the Great Tribulation, the death of the beast in Revelation catches us off guard. How does Antichrist live to rule the world during the Great Tribulation?

### Can the Devil Duplicate the Resurrection of Christ?

J. Vernon McGee answers this question directly:

Nobody can duplicate the resurrection of Christ; they might imitate it, but they cannot duplicate it. Yet Antichrist is going to imitate it in a way that will fool the world—it is the big lie.[13]

Some futurists say that the beast will be brought back from the realm of the dead "by permitted Satanic agency."[14] Resurrection, however, is the great evidence of Christ's deity. Jesus Christ was "declared to be the Son of God with power according to the Spirit of holiness, by the resurrection from the dead" (Rom. 1:4). For this reason, the idea that God would grant Satan power to raise the dead should be dismissed.

If Antichrist actually dies and Satan cannot raise him from the dead, how are we to understand his return to life? Some futurists maintain that the beast's resurrection is a counterfeit without saying how this is accomplished. Gregory Harris argues that the beast and false prophet are human beings who die, undergo the supernatural transformation by which the unsaved receive bodies fit for eternal damnation, and then operate in these supernatural bodies during the Great Tribulation.[15] Futuristic traditionalists offer various explanations but no satisfactory answer. Harris affirms the reality of the beast's death without ascribing undue power to Satan, but the idea that Antichrist and the false prophet receive bodies fit for eternal misery in hell, in accordance with traditionalism, and subsequently spend three-and-a-half years ruling the world is highly unlikely. Solving the mystery of the beast's return to life will require another of John's exclusive revelations.

## The Abyss Factor

Another prophetic truth exclusive to Revelation is that Antichrist will ascend out of the abyss, or bottomless pit. We are first informed that the beast will ascend out of the abyss in Revelation 11:7: "When they [God's two witnesses] finish their testimony, *the beast that ascends out of the bottomless pit* will make war against them, overcome them, and kill them." The timing of Antichrist's ascension from the abyss is significant; it occurs after his death, as an angel indicates to John: "The beast that you saw was, and *is not*, and will ascend out of the bottomless pit" (Rev. 17:8). Robert Thomas writes,

> The designation of the beast as the one who "was and is not, and is about to ascend out of the abyss" ... ties him to the beast with the death-wound who was healed in 13:3, 12, 14. Both there and here the earth-dwellers express amazement (Johnson). The words "is not" refer to the

beast's death, and his ascent from the abyss means he will come to life again (cf. 13:14).[16]

The abyss is highly significant to our understanding of the beast. It literally means "unfathomably deep"[17] and is a place of confinement for demonic spirits. In Luke, demons beg Jesus not to send them into the abyss (8:31), where Satan will be confined during the millennial reign of Christ (Rev. 20:1–3). In Revelation 9:1–11, demonic locust beings are released from the abyss to torment those who do not have the seal of God on their foreheads. Thomas writes,

> Heavy evidence favors the identification of these locusts as demons or fallen angels ... They have an angel as their leader (9:11). They come from the abyss where evil spirits are imprisoned (Beckwith, Lenski). Their attack against men rather than consuming of green vegetation points to their demonic nature (Beasley-Murray). They have a form such as no human being has ever seen (Bullinger, Seiss, Walvoord).[18]

In Revelation 20:7–8, Satan is released from the abyss to draw out the rebels from among the nations at the end of the millennium. Are we not also to understand that a demonic spirit ascends out of the abyss to assume the identity of the beast?

## THE IDENTITY OF THE BEAST

If we put these two new revelations together—the slaying of Antichrist and his ascension from the abyss—what is the obvious conclusion? When the evil "prince who is to come" suffers a deathblow, his soul goes to Hades as is customary for the unsaved. The slain prince "lives again" when a demonic spirit ascends out of the abyss to possess and animate the prince's slain body.[19]

This is the one view that accounts for all of the key issues. It satisfies the strong wording of the scripture that the beast actually dies. It takes the beast's ascension out of the bottomless pit at face value. It protects rather than threatens the great evidence of Christ's deity by assuring us that the resurrection of Antichrist is a counterfeit resurrection. It is also consistent with the fact that the unsaved world will marvel.

It is possible that Antichrist's recovery from a deathblow will be witnessed on live TV or some streaming platform, but think of the effect that fingerprints and DNA might provide if a demonic spirit were to possess Antichrist's slain body. Imagine the impact of watching Antichrist pass eye-scan security measures. With scientific verification that death has been conquered, no wonder the unsaved world will marvel and follow Antichrist.[20]

Outwardly and to the world, Antichrist was killed and rose from the dead. People will believe this because of what their eyes see and science verifies, but the world will be deceived; if Antichrist's dead body is resurrected, it will be because a demonic spirit from the bottomless pit possesses it. How is it that futuristic traditionalists have missed this common-sense reading of Revelation? It's surely because seeing two human beings suffering in the lake of fire with Satan is so fundamental to their position on hell that it simply hasn't been a possibility for them.

Let's hope, at the very least, futurists will correct this defective aspect of their eschatology. It would be a great help for those living through the Tribulation to know not only that Antichrist's resurrection is a counterfeit but also how it is accomplished. As of this writing, the vast majority of futurist literature does not contain this crucial insight.

## THE NUMBER OF THE BEAST

The number 666 is well-known in popular culture as being associated with the devil. In Revelation 13, it is the number of the beast, and it is the number of a man (v. 18). Is there a conflict between the true identity of the beast as a fallen angel and the fact that his number is the number of a man? Because the treacherous prince's human form and identity remain intact throughout the Tribulation, it is fitting that Antichrist's number is said to be the number of a man. There is strong scriptural precedent for this conclusion.

### *Spirit Beings in Human Form*

Though angels do not have bodies of flesh that can be seen or handled, they are capable of operating in human form (Heb. 13:2). In Genesis 18, three men visited Abraham in Mamre (vv. 1–2). Abraham's hospitality included providing water to wash the men's feet (v. 4) and food, which the men ate under the shade of a tree (v. 8). Afterward, "the men rose from there and looked toward Sodom, and Abraham went with them to send them on the way" (v. 16). Upon learning of Sodom's impending judgment, Abraham stood before the Lord and talked with Him while two of the men went toward Sodom (v. 22) where some of Abraham's relatives lived. This story continues in Genesis 19, where we learn that the two men are actually angels.

Abraham's nephew Lot greeted the angels (v. 1) and offered them water for their feet (v. 2) and insisted that they lodge under his roof (v. 3a). Then Lot prepared a meal that the two ate (v. 3b). Before long, the men of Sodom surrounded Lot's house (v. 4), wanting Lot to bring out "the men who came to you tonight" (v. 5). Lot stepped out of his house, shutting the door behind him, in an attempt to protect his guests, but the crowd threatened Lot and were close to breaking his door down when, from within the house, "the men reached out their hands and pulled Lot into the house with them, and shut the door" (v. 10). Then Lot's two guests ended the confrontation by striking the men outside the doorway with blindness (v. 11).

These two angels were in the physical form of men, were recognized as men by all who met them, and performed everyday human tasks. Most significant to our study is the fact that *scripture repeatedly refers to these angels as men.* Since scripture refers to angelic beings in human form as men, it is surely appropriate that the mark of a fallen angel operating in human form is said to be the mark of an evil man.

## THE SATANIC TRINITY

Satan is an imitator who seeks to take the place of God. The devil's ambition to be like the Most High is widely recognized by students of the Bible. In Revelation, we see Satan form an imitation trinity with the beast and false prophet:

> And I saw a beast rising up out of the sea ... The dragon gave
> him his power, his throne, and great authority. (Rev. 13:1–2)

> Then I saw *another* [Gr. *allo* "one like in kind"[21]] beast [aka, the false prophet] coming up out of the earth, and he had two horns like a lamb and *spoke like a dragon*. And he *exercises all the authority of the first beast* in his presence, and causes the earth and those who dwell in it to worship the first beast, whose deadly wound was healed. (Rev. 13:11–12)

Futuristic traditionalists customarily teach that Satan will form his counterfeit trinity with two human beings. The divine Holy Trinity, however, is comprised of coequal Persons. Angels and humans are not equals (2 Pet. 2:11). Because Satan is a fallen cherub, we should expect that he would form his imitation trinity with other fallen angels.

> And I saw three unclean spirits like frogs coming out of the mouth of the dragon, out of the mouth of the beast, and out of the mouth of the false prophet. For they are *spirits of demons*, performing signs, which go out to the kings of the earth and of the whole world, to gather them to the battle of that great day of God Almighty. (Rev. 16:13–14)

Out of the mouth of the dragon, beast, and false prophet come unclean spirits that are explicitly declared to be spirits of *demons*. Is this not a picture of a demonic trio? If we see a satanic trinity in Revelation 16, we should also see the devil and his angels in Revelation 20:10.

## THE SATANIC TRINITY IN REVELATION 20:10

Our investigation discovered that Antichrist and the false prophet are in reality fallen angels. Halfway through the

Tribulation, a demonic spirit ascends out of the abyss to possess Antichrist's slain body. The false prophet is another like Antichrist. In Revelation 20:10, then, we have a picture of the devil and his angels in the fire prepared for them.

If the beast and false prophet, at the end of their time on earth, are not human beings, their experience in the lake of fire does not tell us what ultimately happens to unsaved human beings. Rather than looking to Revelation 20:10 to learn the destiny of the unsaved teachers who taught us to read and write and the unsaved doctors who performed life-saving surgery on our loved ones and the unsaved men who gave their lives on the beaches of Normandy, conditionalists believe that God expects us to look to texts that explicitly address the fate of unsaved humanity. This is why we spent so much time in Matthew's Gospel where the chaff is incinerated (3:12), broad is the way that leads to destruction in the sense of death (7:13), the killing of soul and body in hell is reason to fear God (10:28), tares are gathered and utterly burned up in fire (13:30, 40), the bad fish are thrown away into a furnace of fire (13:47–50), and the falling Stone grinds to powder (21:44).

## REVELATION 20:10–15 – A MISNOMER

Traditionalists treat Revelation 20:10–15 as if it were a unit of scripture. Peterson argues,

> Revelation 20:10 tells us that the devil will be thrown into
> the lake of fire. Five verses later we read that human beings
> will be cast into the same lake of fire. Wouldn't normal

hermeneutics dictate the understanding that human beings
will be heading for eternal torment too?[22]

Linking Revelation 20:10 with Revelation 20:11–15 is so common that even many conditionalists feel that they must deal with these verses as a unit or passage of scripture, but to do so is to misread and mishandle the text. Scripture can change subjects quickly, and it does so in Revelation 20. Revelation 20:7–10 and Revelation 20:11–15 are two distinct passages with two distinct subjects: Satan and his angels, and the unsaved of Adam's race, respectively.

The proximity of the visions hardly relieves the interpreter of the responsibility to assess each passage separately. The lake of fire is common to both visions, but Satan and Adam are very different creations of God. Furthermore, with regard to sin, God has clearly dealt differently with humans than He has with Satan. As noted previously, Jesus died for fallen human beings, but He did not die for fallen angelic beings. We shouldn't assume that a human being's experience in the lake of fire is identical to that of the devil; instead, we should like good Bereans carefully observe what the text actually teaches.

### *The Visions of John: Revelation 19:11–21:2*

In Revelation 19:11 we read, "*Now I saw* heaven opened, and behold, a white horse. And He who sat on him was called Faithful and True, and in righteousness He judges and makes war." In 19:11–16, Jesus is the subject of John's vision.

In Revelation 19:17 we read, "*Then I saw* an angel standing in the sun; and he cried with a loud voice, saying to all the birds that fly in the midst of heaven, 'Come and gather together for the supper of the great God.'" In 19:17–21, the defeat of the beast and his armies is declared.

In Revelation 20:1 we read, "*Then I saw* an angel coming down from heaven, having the key to the bottomless pit and a great chain in his hand." In 20:1–3, we learn that Satan will be bound for a thousand years.

In Revelation 20:4 we read, "*And I saw* thrones, and they sat on them, and judgment was committed to them." In 20:4–6, the focus is the saints' thousand-year reign with Christ. In 20:7–10, we have the last evil act of Satan on earth and his subsequent casting into the lake of fire.

In Revelation 20:11–12 we read, "*Then I saw* a great white throne and Him who sat on it, from whose face the earth and the heaven fled away. And there was found no place for them. And I saw the dead, small and great, standing before God, and books were opened." In 20:11–15, the final judgment of those who died without faith in Christ is recorded.

In Revelation 21:1 we read, "*Now I saw* a new heaven and a new earth."

In Revelation 21:2 we read, "*Then I*, John, *saw* the holy city, New Jerusalem, coming down out of heaven from God, prepared as a bride adorned for her husband."

## A Fundamental Error of Traditionalism

In Revelation 20:7–10, the casting of Satan into the lake of fire and the torment of the satanic trinity are declared. The judgment of unbelievers *begins* in Revelation 20:11: "*Then I saw* a great white throne." The importance of this simple fact should not be minimized. Revelation 20:10 is *not* the first verse of what God has to say about the judgment of humanity; nevertheless, traditionalists link Revelation 20:10 with Revelation 20:11–15 as if this were the case.

Peterson writes, "Arguably the second most important passage on the doctrine of hell (after Mt 25:41, 46) is Revelation 20:10–15."[23] Citing Revelation 20:10–15 as the second most important *passage* of scripture about hell fails to respect the distinction between the separate visions of Revelation 20:7–10 and Revelation 20:11–15. This is a fundamental error of traditionalism. Torment is not the penalty for sin established in Eden, and torment does not appear in John's vision of unsaved humanity in Revelation 20:11–15. To support their theology, traditionalists assign torment foretold for the satanic trinity in one vision to humankind in another vision. This is not responsible hermeneutics.

## REVELATION 20:7–10 & 20:11–15 PLAYING ON A SPLIT PROPHECY SCREEN

To best appreciate verses 7–10 and 11–15 of Revelation 20, begin by imagining a huge split screen in the sky upon which two movies are playing. On one side of the screen, Satan and his angels are being tormented without relief; on the other side, those who died without Christ face final judgment.

Satan contributed to Adam's fall (Gen. 3:1–7) and works to prevent sinners from coming to faith in Christ (2 Cor. 4:3–4). Thus, it is completely fitting that Satan and his angels should suffer while the judgment of Revelation 20:11–15 takes place.

Every unsaved individual will be judged in accordance with his or her words (Matt. 12:36–37), deeds (Rom. 2:5–6), secrets (Rom. 2:16), and privilege (Lk. 12:48). How long it will take to complete the Great White Throne judgment is not revealed, but it could be a staggering length of time. The church, comprised of finite human beings, will be involved in this judgment (1 Cor. 6:2), and potentially billions of unsaved lives will come before God's throne. As thoroughly deserved, Satan and his angels will suffer throughout the judgment of each and every unbeliever.

Satan's suffering will be continual while the unsaved from throughout the ages stand before the Great White Throne, but his suffering will not necessarily last eternally. "Forever and ever," as previously discovered, requires contextual investigation to determine whether or not eternity is in view. As becoming a servant *forever* to a fellow Israelite (Deut. 15:12–17) lasts for a generation, and the territory given to Israel *forever* (Gen. 13:15) remains her promised land while this earth endures, and the smoke rising from Babylon *forever and ever* (Rev. 19:3) ascends until the city can no longer be found, it certainly would be well within the biblical norm if the *forever and ever* torment of the devil, beast, and false prophet terminates with the passing away of the present universe.

## IS THERE A PLACE FOR SATAN AND HIS ANGELS IN THE NEW HEAVENS?

One can be a conditionalist and believe that Satan and the fallen angels will suffer ECT. Conditional immortality is a doctrine about human beings; it is only Adam's race that is offered immortality on the condition of faith in the Lord Jesus Christ. A potential problem with Satan and the fallen angels being part of God's new eternal universe is its righteous nature.

The writer of Hebrews links God as *consuming* fire (Heb. 12:29) with the day when God will "shake not only the earth, but also heaven" (Heb. 12:26), resulting in the "removal of those things that are being shaken … that the things which cannot be shaken may remain" (Heb. 12:27). What cannot be shaken is the kingdom of God (Heb. 12:28), which includes heavenly Jerusalem, the holy angels, the church of the firstborn who are registered in heaven, the spirits of just men made perfect, the new covenant, and the shed blood of Christ (Heb. 12:22–24). Neither the devil nor demons have any part in the one and only unshakable kingdom. Since it is God's kingdom alone that will remain, and since Satan and his angels have no part in it, many conditionalists believe that demonic beings will not have a place in the universe to come; I give this just a brief mention because our concern is for human beings and what ultimately happens to them in the flames of *Gehenna*.

## REVELATION 20:11–15 IN A NUTSHELL

The unsaved will be resurrected to stand before God's Great White Throne for judgment. Wrongs in this world will be brought to light as the deeds and secrets of unsaved humanity recorded in the books of heaven are made public (Rev. 20:11–12). No member of Adam's race will be lost to eternal death without a review of his or her life that will affirm that the penalty for sin is deserved. The effort put into this judgment reflects the importance of people to God and the need for closure. Every unsaved sinner will be accounted for, even those lost at sea (20:13).

"Then Death and Hades were cast into the lake of fire. This is the second death" (20:14). Death will be no more (Rev. 21:4), and Hades, an intermediate state, will also be no more. This is arresting because annihilation appears to be set before the reader immediately prior to the words "And anyone not found written in the Book of Life was cast into the lake of fire" (20:15).

We witness the execution of the Genesis 2:17 penalty for sin as the unsaved are cast into the lake of fire, which is the second death. It is unnecessary for the book of Revelation to elaborate, the penalty for sin having already been unequivocally declared. The fire of which Jesus and His forerunner both warned *burns up* chaff and tares, the unsaved of Adam's race.

## CHAPTER SIX

# THE CHURCH AT A CROSSROADS

*D*iscovering the truth of conditional immortality resolved a conflict that had long been buried deep inside of me. It was an incredible relief to know that God did not sentence mothers and fathers and sons and daughters to eternal suffering. This world was no longer a treacherous danger zone that could send a person into a nightmare beyond comprehension. God's creation of human beings and the earth itself was truly good. I sensed His goodness with every fiber of my being and was filled with peace. If *Eternal by Choice* has deepened your appreciation of God's goodness, my purpose in writing it has been fulfilled, in part.

ECT doctrine is not only a terrible error rooted in Greek philosophy that creates anguish in people, it has had a devastating effect on the mission of the church. We need to recognize the damage done by the traditional view of hell to the work of the Great Commission and discover how conditionalism can strengthen believers to stand strong in these last days.

# ECT'S ROLE IN THE RISE OF SECULAR UNIVERSALISM

A contestant is about to perform on one of the many talent reality shows that are so popular today. The performer dedicates her performance to a loved one who recently died. How do non-Christian celebrity judges typically respond? They affirm that the contestant's loved one is watching from above and very proud of her. How did universalism come to prominence in our present secular world? Do evangelicals bear some responsibility?

Consider the messaging that the world has heard from evangelicals. Simply put, we've led with two main points: God is love, and everyone lives somewhere forever. The third point, of course, is that one must choose Christ to go to heaven. It seems, however, that many never get past the two leading points. This shouldn't surprise us.

If God is love and everyone lives forever, what is there to worry about? The secularist simply can't imagine anyone being sentenced to an eternity of torment by a God of love. So if everyone lives forever, virtually everyone must make it into a better existence. This leaves secularists free to do their own thing without fear of punishment. Many take comfort in the modern traditionalist message being broadcast by the church while ignoring and even attacking biblical values.

## A REASON TO LISTEN AND BELIEVE

Unsaved people need a reason to listen to the Gospel and give it the consideration it deserves. Traditionalism's "God is love and everyone lives forever" message does not provide that, but the doctrine of conditional immortality does.

Scripture says that people are "held in slavery by their fear of death" (Heb. 2:15, NIV). This truth has been on full display during the COVID-19 pandemic. The loss of freedom, isolation and depression, and other devastating effects resulted from the fear of a virus. People know death is coming for them; they fear it and long for a solution to it. That Jesus conquered death by His sacrifice at Calvary and His bodily resurrection from the tomb gives Christianity immense value. Indeed, having the answer to death is the great leverage that God has given the church. What have evangelicals done with this advantage? Tragically, we have squandered it.

To the unsaved who have a profound need for an answer to death, evangelicals have proclaimed loudly and clearly that everyone is going to live forever. Why undermine our advantage? Why try to erase the central problem of humanity that Christianity alone has the answer to, especially considering the times we are living in? Things seem to get worse overnight. Some sins are now considered a noble cause to be supported; good is being called evil. Christianity is rapidly losing relevance, but it doesn't have to be this way. The apostles also faced opposition; let's look at the message they proclaimed.

## THEY PREACHED JESUS AND HIS RESURRECTION

ECT theology is conspicuous in the book of Acts only by its absence; there is not a word about it. What is repeatedly mentioned in *The Acts of the Apostles* is the resurrection of Christ. When talking about the need for someone to take Judas' apostolic position, Peter cites being a witness to Christ's resurrection as the ministry of the apostles (1:15–25). In Acts 4:33, we read that "with great power the apostles gave witness to the resurrection of the Lord Jesus." The good news preached by Paul centered on two main points: Christ died for our sins as evidenced by the fact that He was buried; Jesus rose bodily from the tomb as evidenced by His being seen by many people after His crucifixion (1 Cor. 15:1–8). The importance of the resurrection can hardly be overstated. It declares the deity of Christ (Rom. 1:4), guarantees that there will be a final judgment (Acts 17:30–31), and assures our victory over death (Jn. 11:25, 14:19). It is also crucial to believers standing strong in these last days.

Paul concludes the magnificent fifteenth chapter of First Corinthians with these words: "Therefore, my beloved brethren, be steadfast, immovable, always abounding in the work of the Lord, knowing that your labor is not in vain in the Lord" (v. 58). What truth should enable believers to be steadfast and immovable? In the previous forty-plus verses, Paul emphasized one thing: the resurrection of Christ.

Because Christ was resurrected, believers in Jesus will "put on immortality" so that "death is swallowed up in victory" (1 Cor. 15:54). This is our sustaining hope. No matter what the world throws at us, we have the answer to life's paramount problem. We should boldly proclaim it. This is not only pragmatically wise; it is our Great Commission duty. This will require new witnessing resources to share with the world. Here, for example, are five principles that a Gospel tract could be built upon.

1. The eternal Son of God became a man, Jesus of Nazareth, in order to rescue us from death (Jn. 1:1–14, 6:47–51).

2. Death exists and is coming for us all because all have sinned and fall short of the glory of God (Rom. 3:19, 6:23).

3. God sent His Son to die for our sins and rise from the dead because He loves us and wants us to have eternal life (Jn. 3:16; 1 Cor. 15:1–8).

4. Those that receive Christ become members of God's forever family and will live in harmony with Him on a new earth where there will be no more death nor sorrow nor pain (Jn. 1:12; Rev. 21:1–4).

5. All who refuse God's offer of reconciliation will perish; their lives will end. This is plainly appropriate, for one cannot reject his or her Creator and expect to enjoy the privilege of life in the Creator's universe (Jn. 3:16).

## *People Need to Know that Their Very Existence Depends on Their Response to Christ*

Jesus spoke of hell and the importance of not going there in dramatic, graphic terms. His shocking warnings of hell are intended to get our attention and make us realize that eternal loss of life is to be taken seriously. The lake of fire is where the eternal death of the unsaved takes place. Fire, or the power it represents, is the means of accomplishing the bottom-line reality that Paul faithfully declared: "The wages of sin is death." All people need to know that their very existence is at stake. God put the desire to live in the human heart, and the Gospel intentionally meets this need. We should be cooperating with the Lord, not working against Him.

## WILL THE CHURCH COME TO ITS EVANGELISTIC SENSES?

We often hear traditionalists say that the need for justice demands Eternal Conscious Torment, as if no other alternative existed. What perfect justice truly requires is a *fair and just penalty* for sin. The traditional view of hell is neither fair nor just; by changing the meaning of death to eternal misery, ECT theology transforms the Good News of the Gospel into Horrific News for the impenitent and all who care about them. This is tragic not only because God is misrepresented and His love obscured but because it impedes evangelism.

Given how horrific the thought of mothers and fathers and sons and daughters endlessly suffering is, should we be surprised if the world rejects the Gospel? C. S. Lewis wrote that the traditional view of hell is "one of the chief grounds on which Christianity is attacked as barbarous, and the goodness of God impugned."[1] When Lewis wrote this in 1940, the church still had a strong influence in most of Western Civilization. In our largely unchurched post-Christian society, evangelicals don't have the benefit of most people being indoctrinated in Christianity from birth. We have to earn the right to be heard, and what we say must be worthy of being heard.

Two paths are before us: We can maintain a penalty for sin that the secular world doesn't take seriously because it's inconceivable, or we can read John 3:16 with the heart of a child and provide humanity with the answer to a profound concern that everyone longs for a solution to.

## THE CATCH-22 THAT SUSTAINS ECT

The late nineteenth and early twentieth century saw an assault on the scriptures that eventually produced our modern secular society. The three driving factors of liberalism were Darwinian evolution, comparative religion, and higher criticism. David O. Beale writes,

> Evolution attacked the biblical account of creation, as well as bringing into question the depravity of man and the significance of the work of Christ. Comparative religion attacked the uniqueness of Christianity as the way of salvation and the need for divine revelation. Biblical criticism attacked the integrity and historicity of Scripture.[2]

It was in the midst of the turmoil and controversy brought about by the rise of liberalism that the doctrinal statements of most American evangelical Bible colleges and seminaries were formulated. Since the liberals attacking the Christian faith typically also rejected the traditional view of hell, it was common for these doctrinal statements to affirm ECT theology. The desire to guard against liberal encroachment is understandable, but it had a terrible consequence.

Because Christian schools usually require that their doctrinal statements be affirmed by faculty members, the inclusion of ECT means that many Bible college and seminary professors are not free to consider the conditional immortality understanding of hell without jeopardizing their employment. Indeed, unless one is truly prepared to lose his or her dream job, it is difficult to see how the faculty members of conservative evangelical schools can consider conditionalism with the heart of a Berean.

In 2012, I sent print copies of the original *Rescue from Death* to a number of evangelicals. After the 2017 second edition of *Rescue* was finished, I sent hundreds of electronic copies across the country. Interestingly, in both cases, those with jobs on the line tended not to acknowledge receiving *Rescue*. In contrast, those without jobs on the line tended to respond with thankfulness and positive feedback.

One professor, loved and respected by many after over forty years of teaching Bible and Theology at a well-known evangelical school, shared that he hadn't taken time to seriously grapple with final punishment until after he had retired. He had chosen to focus on other issues because further investigation into hell might result in his not being able to sign the doctrinal statement. The blunt reality, as he called it, of having to sign the doctrinal statement not only inhibited his willingness to rethink hell while employed but in retirement also made him hesitant to ask colleagues yet under contract to join him in taking a closer look at the subject, even though he now had serious reservations about the scriptural basis for ECT. What a predicament.

A proper examination of hell requires the freedom to believe whatever scripture affirms, but conservative evangelical schools threaten to terminate the employment of teachers who take verses such as John 3:16 at face value. This same situation is also true in many Christian ministries and churches. Might this help explain why ECT continues to be the dominant view in conservative evangelical circles in our own day?

## WILL THE CHURCH HEED JESUS' JOHN 17 PRAYER?

I've wanted to see evangelical institutions reject ECT and embrace conditionalism in doctrinal statements, but as terrible an error as I believe ECT to be, the fact remains that many were indoctrinated in ECT theology at a young age by believers who had themselves been likewise trained. We should keep this in mind, especially if conditionalism becomes the dominant view. I don't want to see traditionalists fired or denied employment. We can well afford to be charitable to our traditionalist brethren, trusting that the truth about hell will be evident where the opportunity to freely discuss the biblical texts is allowed.

There has been a greater recognition in recent years that we shouldn't allow secondary issues to divide us, yet many schools and churches continue to do so. I think unity, research, and a Berean spirit would be best served if Bible colleges, seminaries, and churches left final judgment out of doctrinal statements. Wouldn't this be in keeping with the prayers of Jesus for believers that "they may be perfected in unity, so that the world may know that You sent Me" (Jn. 17:23, NASB)?

At the very least, language in doctrinal statements should be adopted that is general enough to allow for conditionalism or ECT. Right now, the list of evangelical schools, ministries, and churches that shut out conditionalists from employment and membership is long. If you believe this needs to change, will you speak up? Every voice matters. Will yours be heard?

## CHANGE REQUIRES ACTION

If evangelical schools and churches have ECT in their doctrinal statements, they don't have to do anything to maintain the status quo; they can simply ignore or put off any discussion of conditionalism and things will stay the way they are. Change requires effort; it doesn't happen unless people act. Someone has to get a conversation going. We need modern-day reformers who are willing to bring their local community of believers together to take a fresh look at final judgment. And it's not too difficult; it can be as simple as: (a) I think we have made an evangelistic mistake that needs to be corrected; (b) the problem and solution are spelled out in *Eternal by Choice*; (c) let's read *EBC* and reset our outreach to the world.

## A SPECIAL OFFER TO RETIRED TEACHERS

Change can be difficult, especially if one has seen things in a particular way for a lifetime, but retired Bible college and seminary teachers are in a unique position to make a difference. You have the respect of a school that should listen to you. If you believe that today's faculty members ought to have greater freedom to explore conditional immortality, contact me through Sherwood Heritage Press;[3] I will do my best to provide copies of *Eternal by Choice* for the key leaders of your school.

## ENCOURAGEMENT TO BIBLE STUDENTS

It breaks my heart to think of Bible college and seminary students being asked to carry ECT theology with them to the frontlines of ministry in today's world. You've been a major inspiration for both *Rescue from Death* and *Eternal by Choice*. Be true Bereans. Ask your professors the tough questions that long have been ignored. Get discussions going with fellow students. You're not just the future leaders of the church; you can be difference-makers today. Please never underestimate the power you have to bring about real reform and revival in the schools you presently attend.

## TO BELIEVERS EVERYWHERE

All of us have a role to play in transmitting God's goodness, love, and justice to the world. Evangelism is the work of the church scattered; it is believers interacting with the world in the course of their everyday lives. No one has a better chance of reaching the lost than a brother or sister in Christ who cares for the unsaved and is willing to share the story of Jesus' death and resurrection. You are the primary reason I wrote *Eternal by Choice*. There are priceless rewards for those who faithfully take His message to the world.

# ENDNOTES

CHAPTER ONE

1    C. S. Lewis, *The Problem of Pain*, Published by Tingle Books, Kindle Version, p95.

2    Ibid., p96.

3    J. I. Packer, "Evangelicals and the Way of Salvation" in *Evangelical Affirmations* (Grand Rapids: Zondervan, 1990), citation by Albert Mohler, "Modern Theology: The Disappearance of Hell" in *Hell under Fire*, Christopher W. Morgan and Robert A. Peterson, General Editors (Grand Rapids: Zondervan, 2004), p32.

4    Ibid.

5    Francis Chan and Preston Sprinkle, *Erasing Hell* (Colorado Springs: David C. Cook, 2011), pp107–108.

6    John Stott, *Essentials: A liberal-evangelical dialogue*, by David L. Edwards with John Stott (London: Hodder & Stoughton, 1988), p314.

7    I went to Multnomah because of its founder, Dr. Mitchell. When it comes to understanding the Bible, no one has had a bigger impact on me. The time I spent with him during the last summer of his life is among my most treasured memories.

8    John Stott, *Essentials: A liberal-evangelical dialogue*, p320.

9    John F. Walvoord, *The Revelation of Jesus Christ* (Chicago: Moody Press, 1966), p307.

10   In *Rescue from Death*, I quoted the *International Standard Bible Encyclopaedia*, which holds that what happens in the intermediate state isn't clearly revealed by the New Testament: "The NT places the emphasis on the eschatological developments at the end, and leaves many things connected with the intermediate state in darkness" (Geerhardus Vos, "Hades," *ISBE*, Vol II, Eerdmans Publishing Co., 1939, p1315). Reviewing what the Old Testament says about *Sheol* for this book has convinced me that an active

conscious existence is not the *norm* for Hades. Psalm 115:17 informs us that the dead go down into silence. Similarly, Psalm 94:17 states, "If the Lord had not been my help, My soul would soon have dwelt in the land of silence" (NASB). The Preacher tells us that "there is no work or thought or knowledge or wisdom in Sheol" (Ecc. 9:10, ESV). Job called Sheol a place of quiet, rest, and sleep (Job 3:11–19).

Punishment rightly follows a just trial, and the Bible clearly teaches that Hades delivers those held there to stand before God's Great White Throne where they will be judged according to their works (Rev. 20:11–13). To receive punishment prior to this trial seems inappropriate. What, then, was Jesus' purpose in telling the story of the rich man and Lazarus?

Like myself, many *traditionalists* believe that the purpose was to warn of the dangers of riches. Lovers of money (Lk. 16:14), the Pharisees saw themselves as Abraham's heirs (Matt. 3:9; Jn. 8:33, 39) but did not walk in Abraham's ways (Jn. 8:39–41). Rather than live by faith in God's Word as Abraham had (Gen. 15:1–6), the Pharisees demanded miraculous works of Christ (Jn. 6:30). Contextually, then, in light of the Pharisees' scoffing at Jesus' teaching that one cannot serve both God and money (Lk. 16:13–14), the rich man ending up in flames of torment and the beggar finding solace in Abraham's bosom are a powerful rebuke to the Pharisaic view that wealth is an indication of God's favor.

Jesus also seems to be saying that salvation belongs to those who believe God's Word. This is seen in the parable's conclusion: "If they do not hear Moses and the prophets, neither will they be persuaded though one rise from the dead" (Lk. 16:31). It is with good reason, then, that many believe that the story of the rich man and Lazarus was crafted to address issues of this world, namely, the Pharisees' materialism, self-righteousness, and unbelief.

I don't think we should be dogmatic about Hades. Whatever the case may be, Hades is a temporary situation for the unsaved. The far more important question is what ultimately happens to the unsaved in hell.

11   Christopher W. Morgan, "Biblical Theology: Three Pictures of
     Hell," *Hell under Fire*, p147.

12   Basil Atkinson, *Life and Immortality*, Chapter 4, "Unquenchable
     Fire,"https://lifebeyonddeath.wordpress.com/2013/11/25/life-
     and-immortality-by-basil-atkinson/. Accessed July 23, 2022.

     Atkinson (1895–1971) had a key role in the formation of Inter-
     Varsity Fellowship of Evangelical Unions.

## CHAPTER TWO

1    David C. Needham, *Close to His Majesty* (Portland: Multnomah
     Press, 1987), p89.

2    John H. Sailhamer, "Genesis," *The Expositor's Bible Commentary*,
     Vol. 2, Frank E. Gaebelein, General Editor (Grand Rapids:
     Zondervan Publishing House, 1990), p48.

3    *Talk Genesis*, "Why didn't Adam die the day he ate?", Nov. 3, 2015,
     http://www.talkgenesis.org/why-didnt-adam-die-the-day-he-ate/.

4    *Rethinking Hell*, "Statement on Evangelical Conditionalism,"
     https://rethinkinghell.com/statement/. Accessed July 23, 2022.

5    Of *thnesko*, W. E. Vine states, "To die (in the perf. tense, to be
     dead), in the N.T. is always used of physical death, except in
     I Timothy 5:6, where it is metaphorically used of the loss of
     spiritual life" (*An Expository Dictionary of New Testament
     Words*, Vol I [Old Tappan: Fleming H. Revell Co, 1966], p308).

     Of *anairesis*, Vine states, "Another word for death ... as of the
     taking of a life, or putting to death; it is found in Acts 8:1, of
     the murder of Stephen" (Ibid., p276).

     Of *teleute*, Vine states, "An end, limit ... hence, the end of life,
     death, is used of the death of Herod, Matt. 2:15" (Ibid., p276).

     *Thanatos* is translated as *death*, e. g., "Now brother will deliver
     up brother to *death*" (Matt. 10:21); "I persecuted this Way to
     the *death*" (Acts 22:4); "And there were many priests, because
     they were prevented by *death* from continuing" (Heb. 7:23).

*Apothnesko* is primarily rendered as *die* or *died*, e. g., "When he [a nobleman] heard that Jesus had come out of Judea into Galilee, he went to Him and implored Him to come down and heal his son, for he was at the point of *death*.... The nobleman said to Him, 'Sir, come down before my child *dies*!'" (Jn. 4:47–49); "For scarcely for a righteous man will one *die*; yet perhaps for a good man someone would even dare to *die*. But God demonstrates His own love toward us, in that while we were still sinners, Christ *died* for us" (Rom. 5:7–8).

It is unfortunate that many believers have been conditioned by traditionalism to think of death in terms of separation. The Bible overwhelmingly speaks of death in its ordinary sense—the absence or cessation of life.

6    Ignatius, *The Epistle of Ignatius to the Magnesians*, Chapter 10, http://www.newadvent.org/fathers/0105.htm. Accessed July 23, 2022.

Contrary to common traditionalist rhetoric, there was no consensus on hell in the early centuries of church history. The reality is that the dominance of the eternal-torment view formed in conjunction with the development of Roman Catholicism. See Chapter 4 ("About Church Tradition").

7    Henry Clarence Thiessen, *Introductory Lectures in Systematic Theology* (Grand Rapids: Wm. B. Eerdmans Publishing Company, 1949), p271.

8    Robert A. Peterson and Edward William Fudge, *Two Views of Hell: A Biblical and Theological Dialogue* (Downers Grove: InterVarsity Press, 2000), p147.

Peterson is a leading proponent of traditionalism. Fudge labored for decades, arguing for conditionalism. He is the author of *The Fire That Consumes* (Verdict Publications).

9    Sean McDowell, "Does a Loving God Send People to Hell?", September 2, 2014, https://seanmcdowell.org/blog/does-a-loving-god-send-people-to-hell.

10   Randy Alcorn, *If God Is Good* (Colorado Springs: Multnomah Books, 2009), p310.

11   Some point to the doctrine of the Trinity to justify affirming direct contradictions supposedly found in scripture. To be sure, the Trinity is beyond our comprehension. But it does not involve direct contradiction. The Trinity does not affirm one God and three Gods. It affirms one God and three Persons. Neither is the sovereignty of God and the free will of man contradictory. God sovereignly created people with free will. Those who affirm direct contradictions in scripture unfortunately, and likely unwittingly, follow the world's way of thinking. To better appreciate this, see Francis Schaeffer's trilogy: *The God Who Is There*, *Escape from Reason*, and *He Is There and He Is Not Silent*.

12   Cited by Edward White in *Life in Christ* (London: Hazell, Watson, and Viney, Printers, 1878), p365.

13   Millard J. Erickson, *Christian Theology* (Grand Rapids: Baker Book House, 1985), p613.

14   Norman Shepherd, "Immortality," *The Zondervan Pictorial Encyclopedia of the Bible*, Vol. 3, Merrill C. Tenney, Gen. Editor (Grand Rapids: Regency Reference Library, 1975), p263.

15   Augustine of Hippo, *The City of God*, Book 13, Chapter 24, https://www.newadvent.org/fathers/120113.htm. Accessed July 24, 2022. Italics mine.

16   Ibid., Book 21, Chapter 3, https://www.newadvent.org/fathers/120121.htm. Accessed July 24, 2022. Italics mine.

17   Commenting on Matthew 10:28, Tertullian (A.D. 150 – 225) wrote: "Here, then, we have a recognition of the natural immortality of the soul." (Tertullian, *On the Resurrection of the Flesh*, Chapter 35, http://www.newadvent.org/fathers/0316.htm. Accessed July 24, 2022.) Tertullian's commitment to the immortality of the soul was strong, and it is obvious he did not set this belief aside when reading scripture. In Chapter 34 of *On the Resurrection of the Flesh*, Tertullian wrote: "We, however, so understand the soul's immortality as to believe it "*lost*," not in the sense of destruction, but of punishment, that is, in hell. And if this is the case, then it is not the soul which salvation will

affect, since it is "*safe*" already in its own nature by reason of its immortality (Ibid.).

18　Augustine of Hippo, *The City of God*, Book 13, Chapter 2, Italics mine.

19　Ibid.

20　Ibid., Book 21, Chapter 3.

21　Philip E. Hughes, *The True Image* (Grand Rapids: Wm. B. Eerdmans Publishing Company, 1989), citation from *Rethinking Hell: Readings in Evangelical Conditionalism*, Christopher M. Date, Gregory G. Stump, and Joshua W. Anderson, Editors (Eugene: Cascade Books, 2014), p192.

22　*Westminster Confession of Faith*, Chapter IV: Of Creation.

23　Clark H. Pinnock, "The Destruction of the Finally Impenitent," *Criswell Theological Review* 4.2 (1990), citation from *Rethinking Hell: Readings in Evangelical Conditionalism*, p67.

## CHAPTER THREE

1　M. R. Vincent, *Word Studies in the New Testament*, Vol. 1 (Mac Dill AFB: MacDonald Publishing Co., n. d.), p31.

2　Paul Enns, *The Moody Handbook of Theology* (Chicago: Moody Press, 1989), p375.

3　Francis A. Schaeffer, *He is There and He is Not Silent* (Wheaton: Tyndale House Publishers, 1972), pp7–8.

4　Ibid., p7.

5　Ibid., p8.

6　Alan W. Gomes, "Evangelicals and the Annihilation of Hell," *Christian Research Journal*, Spring 1991, p18.

7　*Rescue from Death: The Good News of John 3:16* (Sherwood Heritage Press, 2021), pp133–138.

8　A. Oepke, "*apollymi*," *Theological Dictionary of the New Testament*, Gerhard Kittle and Gerhard Friedrich, Editors, Abridged in one volume by Geoffrey W. Bromiley (Grand Rapids:

William B. Eerdmans Publishing Co., 1985), p67. Note: The Greek letter Upsilon can be transliterated either with "u" or "y"; hence, both *apollumi* and *apollymi* are acceptable.

9    Douglas J. Moo, "Paul on Hell," *Hell under Fire*, p105.

10   W. E. Vine, *An Expository Dictionary of New Testament Words*, Vol. I, p159.

11   Alfred Marshall, *The Interlinear Greek-English New Testament* (Grand Rapids: Zondervan Publishing House, 1958), p57.

12   Harold E. Guillebaud, *The Righteous Judge*, Chapter 4, Subsection "Separation from God: Penal Suffering," https://lifebeyonddeath. wordpress.com/2013/11/12/the-righteous-judge-by-harold-e-guillebaud/. Accessed July 29, 2022.

13   Alan W. Gomes, "Annihilation of Hell," *Christian Research Journal*, Summer 1991, p11.

14   Ibid.

15   Robert A. Peterson, *Two Views of Hell*, pp109–110.

16   Randy Alcorn, *If God Is Good* (Colorado Springs: Multnomah Books, 2010), p312.

17   Ibid., 314.

18   Alan W. Gomes, "Evangelicals and the Annihilation of Hell," p17.

19   Ibid., p18.

20   E. Earle Ellis, "New Testament Teaching on Hell" in *Eschatology in Bible & Theology* (Forth Worth: IRLBR, 1999), citation from *Rethinking Hell: Readings in Evangelical Conditionalism*, p132.

## CHAPTER FOUR

1    Francis A. Schaeffer, *Escape from Reason* (Downers Grove: InterVarsity Press, 1968), p26.

2    C. S. Lewis, Mere Christianity (Las Vegas: Valde Books, 2021), p27.

3    SBLGNT stands for Society of Biblical Literature Greek New Testament; YLT stands for Young's Literal Translation.

4    Robert W. Yarbrough, "Jesus on Hell," *Hell under Fire*, pp73–74.

5    Robert A. Peterson, *Two Views of Hell*, p150.

6    Ibid.

7    Ibid., pp150–151.

8    Francis Chan and Preston Sprinkle, *Erasing Hell*, p133.

9    Ibid., p134.

10   Ibid., p163.

11   Henry Constable, *The Duration and Nature of Future Punishment*, Fifth Edition (London: Kellaway & Co., 1875), p138.

12   Ibid., pp138–139.

13   Francis Chan and Preston Sprinkle, *Erasing Hell*, p149.

14   Ibid., pp132–133, 138.

15   Edward William Fudge, *Two Views of Hell*, p193.

16   John H. Yoder and Alan Kreider, "The Anabaptists," *Eerdmans' Handbook to the History of Christianity* (Grand Rapids: Wm. B. Eerdmans Publishing Co., 1977), p401.

17   Ibid., 402.

18   John G. Stackhouse Jr., "Foreword," *Rethinking Hell: Readings in Evangelical Conditionalism*, pxii.

This collection of conditionalist writings was put together by the Rethinking Hell project. Check out rethinkinghell.com for additional helpful resources.

19   *The Nature of Hell*: A Report by the Evangelical Alliance Commission on Unity and Truth among Evangelicals (ACUTE), David Hilborn, Editor (Carlisle: Paternoster Press, 2000), "Conclusions and Recommendations," Number 19, citation from https://www.eauk.org/church/resources/theological-articles/upload/The-Nature-of-Hell-2.pdf. Accessed July 31, 2022.

20   https://www.gotquestions.org/conditional-immortality.html. Accessed July 31, 2022.

21   Henry M. Morris, *The Bible Has the Answer* (Grand Rapids: Baker Book House, 1971), p43.

22   Robert A. Peterson, *Two Views of Hell*, p175.

23   William R. Newell, *Romans Verse by Verse* (Iowa Falls: World Bible Publishers, 1987), p173. (Originally published by Moody Press, Chicago, 1938.)

24   Ibid., p208.

25   Arthur D. Jackson, *New Testament Mysteries* (Bemidji: Focus Publishing, 1996), pp114–116.

Commenting on the fact that there will be no sea in the new earth, Henry Morris writes,

The present sea is needed, as was the original antediluvian sea, as a basic reservoir for the maintenance of the hydrologic cycle and the water-based ecology and physiology of the animal and human inhabitants of the earth. In the new earth ... presumably all the men and women who live there will have glorified bodies with no more need of water. Their resurrected bodies will be composed, like that of the Lord Jesus, of flesh and bone (Luke 24:39; Philippians 3:21) but apparently with no need of blood (1 Corinthians 15:50) to serve as a cleanser and restorer of the body's flesh as at present. This, in turn, eliminates the major need for water on the earth (blood is about 90 percent water, and present-day human flesh about 65 percent water). (*The Revelation Record*, Tyndale House Publishers, 1983, p437)

## CHAPTER FIVE

1   Gregory K. Beale, "The Revelation on Hell," *Hell under Fire*, p134.

2   Edward William Fudge, *Hell a Final Word* (Abilene: Leafwood Publishers, 2012), p145.

Conditionalists come from a variety of backgrounds and theological traditions. Thankfully, we tend to be supportive of one another. There is no better example of this than Edward Fudge. In 2012, not long after the first edition of *Rescue from*

*Death* was published, Edward called to congratulate me on the book. He was excited about *Rescue*, even saying that it was the best book on conditionalism that he had seen in thirty years (Edward's *The Fire That Consumes* came out in 1982). Because I believe in the premillennial return of Christ and His thousand-year Messianic reign on earth, I write about some key passages quite differently than most conditionalists have. Edward, a self-described nondispensational amillennialist, appreciated this, and I hope conditionalists who share his eschatology will as well.

3    I say that New Jerusalem is the *primary* focus of Revelation 21 in part because there is an evangelistic pause in Revelation 21:6–8: Today is the day God freely offers the water of life to him that thirsts (v. 6); two ends are in the balance: life with God as your Father in the new earth or second death in the lake of fire (vv. 7–8). Evangelistic concern is also found in the epilogue. This is especially clear in 22:17: "And the Spirit and the bride say, 'Come!' And let him who hears say, 'Come!' And let him who thirsts come. Whoever desires, let him take the water of life freely." Regarding Revelation 22:11—"He who is unjust, let him be unjust still; … he who is righteous, let him be righteous still"— J. Hampton Keathley III states,

Verse 11, which at first seems fatalistic, is closely related to verse 10, the unsealed character of this book and the imminent return of the Lord. Actually it is evangelistic. It is an appeal to men to respond to this book, for if one does not, there is no other message which can change him. Concerning this verse Walvoord writes: "If the warnings of the book are not sufficient, there is no more that God has to say. The wicked must continue in their wicked way and be judged by the Lord when He comes. The same rule, however, applies to the righteous. Their reaction to the prophecy, of course, will be different, but the exhortation in their case is to continue in righteousness and holiness. It is an either/or proposition with no neutrality possible." (*Studies in Revelation*, Biblical Studies Press, 1997, "The Epilogue," citation from Bible.org, https://bible.org/seriespage/29-epilogue-rev-226-21. Accessed 7/31/2022.)

4    Robert A. Peterson, *Two Views of Hell*, pp159–160.

5    Charles C. Ryrie, *Revelation* (Chicago: Moody Publishers, 1996), p103.

6    H. A. Ironside, *Lectures on the Book of Revelation* (Neptune: Loizeaux Brothers, 1973), pp258–259.

7    Robert A. Peterson, *Two Views of Hell*, p161.

8    W. E. Vine, *An Expository Dictionary of New Testament Words*, Vol. II, p47.

9    Gregory K. Beale, "The Revelation on Hell," *Hell under Fire*, pp128–129.

10   Fritz Rienecker, *A Linguistic Key to the Greek New Testament*, Cleon Rogers, Editor (Grand Rapids: Zondervan, 1976), p844.

11   William R. Newell, *Revelation: Chapter-by-Chapter* (Grand Rapids: Kregel Classics, 1994), p186. (Originally published in 1935 by Grace Publications.)

12   Joseph A. Seiss, *The Apocalypse* (Grand Rapids: Kregel Publications, 1987), p325. (Originally published in 1900 by C. C. Cook.)

13   J. Vernon McGee, *Thru the Bible*, Vol. V (Nashville: Thomas Nelson Publishers, 1983), p1000.

14   William R. Newell, *Revelation: Chapter-by-Chapter*, p188.

15   Gregory H. Harris, "Can Satan Raise the Dead? Toward a Biblical View of the Beast's Wound," *The Master's Seminary Journal*, Spring 2007, pp23–41.

16   Robert L. Thomas, *Revelation 8–22: An Exegetical Commentary* (Chicago: Moody Press, 1995), p292.

17   Fritz Rienecker, *A Linguistic Key to the Greek New Testament*, p832.

18   Robert L. Thomas, *Revelation 8–22: An Exegetical Commentary*, p30.

19   Less probable, though still a possibility, is that a fallen angel might take on a human form similar to that of the slain prince.

In either case, a satanic being ascends out of the abyss to assume the identity of the treacherous end-time prince.

20   This paragraph includes details not recorded in scripture but rather derived from reasonable assumptions based on early twenty-first century reality.

21   John F. Walvoord, *The Revelation of Jesus Christ*, p205.

22   Robert A. Peterson, *Two Views of Hell*, p111.

23   Ibid., 110.

## CHAPTER SIX

1   C. S. Lewis, *The Problem of Pain*, Published by Tingle Books, Kindle Version, p95.

2   David O. Beale, *In Pursuit of Purity: American Fundamentalism Since 1850* (Greenville: Unusual Publications, 1986), p80.

3   sherwoodheritagepress@outlook.com